INSIGHT ⊘ GUIDES

EXPLORE

ITALIAN LAKES

PLAN & BOOK
YOUR TAILOR-MADE TRIP

BRAZIL **CHILE** **ECUADOR**

TAILOR-MADE TRIPS & UNIQUE EXPERIENCES CREATED BY LOCAL TRAVEL EXPERTS AT INSIGHTGUIDES.COM/HOLIDAYS

Insight Guides has been inspiring travellers with high-quality travel content for over 45 years. As well as our popular guidebooks, we now offer the opportunity to book tailor-made private trips completely personalised to your needs and interests.

By connecting with one of our local experts, you will directly benefit from their expertise and local know-how, helping you create memories that will last a lifetime.

HOW INSIGHTGUIDES.COM/HOLIDAYS WORKS

STEP 1

Pick your dream destination and submit an enquiry, or modify an existing itinerary if you prefer.

STEP 2

Fill in a short form, sharing details of your travel plans and preferences with a local expert.

STEP 3

Your local expert will create your personalised itinerary, which you can amend until you are completely satisfied.

STEP 4

Book securely online. Pack your bags and enjoy your holiday! Your local expert will be available to answer questions during your trip.

CONTENTS

ART LOVERS

View rich collections of Renaissance art, from Bergamo's Accademia Carrara (route 11) to Milan's Museo Poldi Pezzoli and Pinacoteca di Brera, home to Leonardo da Vinci's *The Last Supper* (route 18).

RECOMMENDED ROUTES FOR...

CASTLE ENTHUSIASTS

Lake Garda's shores (routes 14 and 15) are studded with medieval castles. Trentino (route 17) is dotted with fortifications, while Angera (route 2) is home to the imposing Rocca Borromeo.

ESCAPING THE CROWDS

Take a dip in unspoilt Lake Mergozzo (route 4), or spend time on the tranquil shores of Lake Iseo (route 12). Relatively unexplored Franciacorta (route 13) is a pretty region for touring.

FERRY TRIPS

Sit back and let the ferries do the work for you. The cruises from Stresa to Locarno (route 5), Como to Bellagio (tour 10) and Sirmione to Malcesine (route 15) are among the most scenic.

FOOD AND WINE

Vinophiles and gourmets will enjoy Franciacorta (route 13), home of Italy's finest sparkling wine and many great restaurants. Bergamo (route 11) is a foodie favourite. The culinary scene in Milan (route 18) caters for all tastes.

ISLAND HOPPING

Follow the crowds to the Borromean Islands (route 1); visit Lake Orta's Isola di San Giulio (route 6), or lunch on Como's Isola Comacina (route 10). Hike or bike around Lake Iseo's Monte Isola (route 12).

SHOPPING

Head to the factory outlets of Como (route 9), 'City of Silk', for discounted designer clothes and accessories; or browse in the boutiques of Bellagio (route 8) or Bergamo (route 11).

VILLAS AND GARDENS

Lake Maggiore's showpiece is Villa Taranto (route 4), while Lake Como boasts villas Carlotta, Melzi and Serbelloni (route 8) and the movie regular Villa del Balbianello (route 10).

INTRODUCTION

An introduction to the Italian Lakes's geography, customs and culture, plus illuminating background information on cuisine, history and what to do when you're there.

Lake Como

EXPLORE THE ITALIAN LAKES

With a mild climate, romantic waterfront views and lush vegetation, the lakes have long been a favoured haunt. Add sports, culture, fashion and gastronomy, and it is little wonder that they remain one of Italy's most popular tourist hotspots.

The deep glacial lakes of northern Italy lie between the southern foothills of the Alps, near the Swiss border, and the low-lying plains of the Po Valley. The famous trio are Lake Como, which lies north of the great metropolis of Milan, Lake Maggiore to the city's northwest and Lake Garda to the east. Although the lakes extend over four regions – Piedmont, Lombardy, Trentino and Veneto – the area is comparatively small and easily covered by car or public transport. The A4 autostrada provides a quick way of getting across the region, and for those who want to explore the shopping delights of Milan, the city is no more than an hour away from Stresa or Como by car or train.

SHAPING THE LAKES

It was glaciers at the end of the last Ice Age that gouged out the ribbons of water that are now the lakes. For over 10,000 years inhabitants have also left their mark on the region, from the prehistoric rock engravings in the Camonica Valley to the remains of Roman villas to the castles and *palazzi*

of the ruling dynasties. The Lombard plain was hardly ideal terrain on which to settle: the marshes needed to be drained and the water channelled into canals. Yet by medieval times it was domesticated and dotted with castles, churches, abbeys and palaces. The transformation, from bog to economic powerhouse, was thanks largely to the industriousness of the lakeside towns' natives and the advent of a prosperous local mercantile class.

LOCAL CULTURE

The lakes region's complex culture can be divided into discrete mini-cultures. The four different regions of the lakes area all have clearly separate identities. But it is the bond with, and loyalty to, their home town that many Italians feel most deeply. The Comaschi (natives of Como), for example, live in close proximity to Milan, one of Europe's great cities, and yet, far from embracing the cosmopolitan life of the city, they identify only with their own town. Members of Como's old commercial families have known each other since infancy, and do business together

Sailing on Lake Garda

in a relaxed way. Their commitment to local culture embraces everything from the local silk industry to an appreciation of the medieval craftsmen who built Como's Romanesque churches. The strong sense of regional identity is also reflected in the host of different dialects and cuisines within the region.

VISITORS TO THE LAKES

The lakes have long cast a spell over visitors. The Romans were enamoured of the lakeside spas – Catullus owned a villa at Sirmione and Pliny the Younger built two villas at Bellagio. Travellers on the Grand Tour, after a treacherous journey over the Alps, were awestruck by the sudden vision of the sublime lakes and the Mediterranean flora that flourished on the shores. Shelley, Wordsworth and other Romantic poets were bewitched by the dramatic natural beauty of the deep-blue waters and mountain peaks. Henry James was almost, but not quite, lost for words:

'On, on into Italy we went – a rapturous progress through a wild luxuriance of corn and olives and figs and mulberries and chestnuts and frescoed villages and clamorous beggars and all the good old Italianisms of tradition.' The sight of sluggish steamers and snow-clad peaks still stirs visitors. But as James said of Lake Como, 'It's the place to enjoy *à deux* – it's a shame to be here in gross melancholy solitude.'

Rich, royal and famous

By the late 19th century the lakes had become a pleasure ground for the rich, royal and famous. In 1879 Queen Victoria stayed at Villa Clara at Baveno on Lake Maggiore. In the same decade Lake Garda – notably the resort of Arco in Trentino – became

A long life in Limone

The citizens of Limone sul Garda on the northwest shore of Lake Garda have one of the highest rates of life expectancy in Europe, with a large number of healthy residents over 80. The absence of heart disease here has been studied by many scientists, who variously ascribe this exceptional healthiness to climate, diet or genes. The village was isolated until the 1930s – only accessible by boat or by crossing the mountains – so the secret may lie in a limited gene pool and rare blood group. A mystery protein in the locals' blood, known as Apolipoprotein A-1 (or Apo A-1 Milano), appears to purge fat from the arteries and give a much reduced susceptibility to heart attacks and strokes. All the carriers are descendants from a couple who married in 1644. Genes aside, a mild climate, stress-free lifestyle and cholesterol-free diet of lemons, lake fish and olives all contribute to the fine health of Lake Garda's residents.

Vineyard in Franciacorta

a retreat for Austrian grand-dukes. While the aristocracy of Mitteleuropa flocked to the sanatoria around Lake Garda, the lake was also appreciated by writers and politicians: the Grand Hotel in Gardone Riviera was patronised by Vladimir Nabokov and Somerset Maugham, and it became Winston Churchill's base for painting holidays.

Celebrity status

Today the lakes provide a weekend or holiday retreat for Milanese industrialists, Russian tycoons and a handful of fashion designers and celebrities. The 'Clooney Effect' (George has a 25-room villa at Laglio) has sent property prices rocketing on the southern shores of Lake Como. The Villa del Balbianello, also on

DON'T LEAVE THE ITALIAN LAKES WITHOUT...

Getting wet. Take a towel and head down to the lake for a swim. Choose from hundreds of kilometres of shoreline and many different lakes. Tiny Lago di Mergozzo is the cleanest of them all. See page 42.

Rewarding yourself with an ice cream. Discover the delicious delights of Italian ice cream at a local gelateria. See page 37.

Partaking in aperitif hour. The after-work happy-hour *aperitivo* has become very much a way of life across much of Italy, and especially around Milan. Stylish bars and cafés serve a sensational range of cocktails, with *stuzzichini* (snacks) and elegant canapés. See page 99.

Sightseeing by boat. Arguably the best way to appreciate the glorious scenery around the lakes is from in the middle of them. Choose from fast or slow options, with the possibility at hopping on and off en route. See page 130.

Reaching the dizzy heights. Take the pain out of climbing the mountains of the lakes by taking a cable car (funicular). All

you have to do is enjoy the views as you go up. See pages 38 and 89.

Sampling some fish from the lakes. So fresh it's almost still flapping, lake fish can be tried as an *antipasto*, in risottos and pasta, and, as a secondo, perhaps simply grilled, baked or fried. See page 81.

Learning about silk. The citizens of Como have manufactured silks, velvets, brocades and damasks since the 16th century. Although silkworms are no longer bred around the lake, Chinese thread is woven and dyed here to the exact specifications of leading Milanese fashion houses. Mantero and Ratti, two of the city's great silk families, supply big-name designers such as Chanel, Dior, Versace and Yves Saint Laurent. On the outskirts of the city is the Museo Didattico della Seta (Museum of Silk; Via Castelnuovo 9; www.museosetacomo.com; Tuesday to Sunday 10am–6pm; charge), which documents the story of Como's silk, covering silkworm-breeding and silk-making.

Castle at Arco

Autumn in Lake Varese

Lake Como, has acquired celebrity status by featuring in a number of blockbuster movies (see page 137). The lakes also feature in the James Bond movie, *Quantum of Solace* which opens with a dramatic car chase in the tunnels along the eastern shore of Lake Garda, culminating in a spectacular crash.

WHICH LAKE?

There are six main holiday lakes, all quite different in character: Orta, Maggiore, Lugano, Como, Iseo and Garda (from west to east). German-orientated Lake Garda is the largest of the lakes and receives the most tourist visitors; its beaches, theme parks, sports and nightlife attract a younger crowd as well as families.

Lake Maggiore – famous for its jewel-like Borromean Islands and mountain-girt northern shores – is the second-largest lake, with its northern section lying in the Swiss canton of Ticino.

Henri-Marie Beyle (better known by his penname, Stendhal) was one of many literati who sang the praises of Lake Maggiore. In a letter to his younger sister in 1811 he wrote, 'When a man has a heart and a shirt he should sell the shirt in order to see Lake Maggiore.'

Lovely little Lake Orta lies to the west, and is noted for its spiritual air and excellent small hotels, while romantic Lake Como, north of Milan, offers dramatic scenery, quaint ports and *belle époque* villas. Captivating and tranquil

Lake Iseo, between lakes Como and Garda, is the region's best-kept secret.

GETTING AROUND

If you are planning to tour a number of lakes, renting a car is certainly the most convenient form of transport. However, driving along the lakeshores is not as leisurely as it may sound. Long stretches of the lakesides, including Como's eastern shore and much of Lake Maggiore's western one, are spoilt by heavy traffic along narrow and tortuous roads. Beware, too, of the dimly lit tunnels along the lakeshores. Cycling is hugely popular in the region, bikes are widely

Villas and gardens

The Baroque period was a golden era for construction; ostentatious villas and gardens embodied the aspirations of ambitious owners. With its landscaped hillside gardens, Villa Carlotta on Lake Como exudes panache, while Lake Maggiore's Isola Bella, its grounds full of statuary, fountains and grottoes, is a triumph of lofty terraces. For the wealthy, there are palatial villas converted to luxury hotels, such as the Villa d'Este at Cernobbio and the Grand Hotel Villa Serbelloni at Bellagio. Wherever you go, the gardens are always sumptuous, with exotic flora that thrives in the benign spring-to-autumn climate.

available for hire and can normally be taken on ferries. An increasing number of hiking routes have opened up, many with ravishing views of the lakes.

Lake trips by boat

Travelling on ferries is the most relaxing way of seeing the lakes. The first steamers on the lakes were launched in 1826, and boats have been ferrying passengers around ever since. In the early days most towns were without a landing stage, and rowing boats used to shuttle passengers and goods to and from the ferries. Today you can cruise around all the main lakes, stopping at almost every village. This is the best way to admire the fine mountain scenery and Riviera-like shores though the recent rise in prices is making it something of a luxury. The enclosed hydrofoils (*aliscafi*), which bypass the smaller ports, are the faster and more expensive means of travel, enabling you to cover the entire length of the larger lakes in 2–3 hours.

Getting high

Mountain cable-cars, whisking you from lakeside towns to mountain summits or ridges, provide another entertaining form of transport, with truly spectacular views. You can take these from Como, Stresa on Lake Maggiore and from Malcesine on Lake Garda. Bergamo has two funiculars, both well worth a trip: one connects the Città Bassa to the Città Alta, climbing 100m (330ft) from Viale Vittorio Emanuele II to the Piazza Mercato delle Scarpe – and taking you 500 years back in time. The other links the Città Alta, beyond the Cittadella, to Colle San Vigilio. From here you can climb to the top of Colle San Vigilio for the Castello, a ruined ancient stronghold, and a public park with fabulous views of Bergamo.

MILAN

Few visitors to the region can resist a day's shopping trip to Milan. The city is synonymous with fashion and packs all the top designer stores in one very exclusive quarter near the centre of the city called the Quadrilatero d'Oro (Golden Quadrangle). But Milan has artistic and architectural treasures as well, among them Leonardo da Vinci's *The Last Supper*, the masterpieces in the Brera Art Gallery and one of the largest and most sumptuous Gothic churches in Europe.

The city underwent infrastructure improvements including a number of cultural projects as it got ready to host EXPO 2015.

OTHER HISTORIC CITIES

The southern stretches of the region are also home to artistically rich cities, such as Bergamo, Brescia, Mantua and Verona. With the exception of Verona, which is internationally renowned for its summer opera festival, which attracts massive numbers of visitors, these

The idyllic setting of Menaggio harbour on Lake Como

historic cities are comparatively free of crowds and commercialism, being bypassed by tourists making a beeline for Italy's more famous destinations. Easily accessed from the lakes, they make ideal destinations for day trips.

TOP TIPS FOR EXPLORING THE ITALIAN LAKES

Trentino logo. When in Trentino, keep an eye out for the 'Osteria Tipica Trentina' signs, indicating restaurants that only serve seasonal local cuisine. These have to offer at least five Trentino cheeses, as well as local wines, grappa and mineral water.

Activities on Como. To take the effort out of arranging your own sports on Lake Como, contact The Orizzonti (www.orizzontilakecomo.com), which organises hiking, cycling and boat tours, horse-riding, caving and many more.

Ticket tip. Note that you can buy a combined entry ticket for both Isola Bella and Isola Madre from either Borromean island; it is cheaper than paying separately to visit each one.

Reserving for lunch. Restaurants in the region typically tend to be very busy, especially at lunchtime, so to avoid having to queue and, at worst, the disappointment of having to miss out altogether (especially if you have your heart set on eating at a particular restaurant), it's recommended to book a table in advance. To dine at one of the area's Michelin-starred restaurants, be sure to book very well in advance. Note that Milan is a business city, so many of its restaurants close all day Saturday and at Sunday lunchtime. If in doubt, check before setting out.

Catching the ferry/ferry timetables. It may sound obvious, but when you consult ferry timetables, do make sure you pick the right ferry for the right day. Unless you are familiar with the leaflets, the differentiation between weekday and Sunday/ holiday travel is not immediately obvious – especially on lakes Como and Iseo. To study timetables online in advance of travel see www.navigazionelaghi.it for Maggiore, Como and Garda, and www.navigazionelagoiseo.it for Iseo.

On your bike. Monte Isola is inundated with visitors in summer and at weekends, but is a delight off-season. You can walk or cycle around the entire island on the lakeshore path (9km/5 miles), or hike up to the island's summit, which commands wonderful lake views. Bikes can be rented from Peschiera Maraglio or Carzano.

Restorative waters. The Italian medical profession insists that the lake climate is beneficial for 'the stressed and neurotic, the arthritic and the asthmatic, the elderly and young children'. As a result, the spas in the region are highly valued, especially those in Sirmione.

Dress appropriately. Remember to dress respectfully if you are visiting churches or other holy places. In some places, this can mean no shorts, mini-skirts or skimpy vest tops.

Mountain cheeses

FOOD AND DRINK

The local cuisine, often enhanced by a mesmerising waterfront setting, is one of the great joys of travelling around the lakes. Regional dishes range from smoked hams and seasoned sausages to creamy risottos and fresh lake fish.

Lombard cuisine is highly varied, with ingredients sourced from lakes, mountains and flatlands. Rice, rather than pasta, is the mainstay of their diet; it is grown on the paddy fields of the Po Valley. Cream is very common, and butter tends to prevail over olive oil in local cooking. Lombardy also produces large quantities of corn, which is made into ubiquitous polenta. However, the lighter ingredients of the Mediterranean diet are also here: abundant fish, fresh fruit and vegetables – plus, of course, a glass or two of red wine.

Each region has its specialities. The Alpine influence can be seen in the array of cheeses, salami, polenta and mushroom dishes on offer in rural inns. The Austrian legacy around the north of Lake Garda has left the locals with a taste for veal, pork, beef, dumplings and gnocchi, while on the southern shore you will find roasts, stews, game and white truffles. Olive oil, oranges, lemons, peaches and pears represent a Mediterranean input. Milan may have moved towards more international tastes, such as sushi, but it still produces the famous *risotto alla milanese*.

PLACES TO EAT

The region is liberally endowed with restaurants, from simple tavernas to temples of gastronomy. These days there is little difference between a *ristorante*, *trattoria or osteria*. The region has many unpretentious *pizzerie*, often offering pasta, meat and fish as well. The best use wood-fired ovens *(forno a legna)*, but these are sometimes open only in the evening. You can often find places serving cheap slices of pizza *(al taglio)*, the favourite Italian takeaway.

Cafés and bars

Cafés are generally referred to in Italian as *bar*, which is actually the counter where coffees are served. Italians frequent bars at all times of day, from the breakfast *cappuccino* and *cornetto* to the late-night liqueur. Standing at the bar *(al banco)* is invariably cheaper than sitting at a table with waiter service. The pre-prandial *aperitivo*, from around 6-9pm, is a way of life in towns and resorts. The price of the drink may seem steep, but snacks, canapés and often a whole buffet are included in the price and can provide a cheap alternative to dinner in a restaurant.

A sample menu   *Dining out in Milan's Brera neighbourhood*

Cafés and bars offer a remarkable range of beverages: Prosecco or *spumante* (Italian sparkling wine, which you can have by the glass), *pirlo* (white wine with Campari or Aperol), Negroni (Campari with vermouth and gin) and a long list of liqueurs and cocktails. An *enoteca* (wine bar) will offer a plate of sliced *proscuitto crudo*, salamis or cheeses to accompany its wide choice of wines.

UPMARKET DINING

You only have to see the stars studded across the region's maps in the Italy Michelin guide to realise how many gourmet restaurants there are here. The settings can be grandiose or minimalist, the food traditional or innovative. Gualtiero Marchesi, who was, before his death, one of Italy's best-known chefs and the first to be awarded three Michelin stars. His legacy lives on in his elegant restaurant, Terrazza Gualtiero Marchesi, with its breath-taking views over Lake Como. His signature dish in life was always *riso, oro e zafferono*, saffron rice topped with a sheet of 24-carat gold leaf. Marchesi, who also ran the Ristorante Teatro alla Scala Il Marchesino in Milan, returned his stars to Michelin, complaining the guide favoured French restaurants over Italian ones. (France has 27 restaurants with three Michelin stars, Italy ten).

To rub shoulders with celebrities, head to Nobu at the Armani emporium in Milan (Via G. Pisoni 1; www.armani.com/restaurant), Il Gatto Nero on Lake Como or the Locanda dell'Isola Comacina (see page 69).

ORDERING YOUR MEAL

Restaurant menus offer four courses: *antipasto*, the starter; *primo*, the first course, which is pasta, risotto or soup; *secondo*, the second course, such as fish or meat (accompanied perhaps by a *contorno*, a vegetable side dish); and finally the *dolce* (dessert), or cheese and coffee. Don't feel pressurised into wading through all four courses; opting for just a couple – and not necessarily the *secondo* – is perfectly acceptable.

WHAT TO EAT

Regional risotto and ravioli

Thanks to the extensive rice fields on the Padua plain, risottos are abundant. Most famous of all, and served throughout the region, is *risotto alla milanese*, made with short-grain Arborio rice, slowly cooked with onions, beef marrow

---

Food and Drink Prices

Throughout this book, we have used the following price guide for a two-course a la carte dinner for one with half a bottle of house wine.

€€€€ = €65 and above
€€€ = €45–65
€€ = €25–45
€ = under €25

Cakes aplenty in a local pasticceria

and stock, served with liberal amounts of butter and Parmesan cheese, and flavoured and coloured with saffron. Rice dishes can be enriched with fish, seafood, meat, wild *porcini* mushrooms, truffles or seasonal vegetables.

The other main *primo* is ravioli, stuffed perhaps with perch and parsley, black truffle, or ricotta or cottage cheese and basil. Look out for *cansonsèi* ravioli from the Bergamo and Brescia regions, or *tortelli di zucca* from Mantua: a sweet-and-sour pasta wrapped around puréed pumpkin and crushed amaretti, served with butter and Grana Padano.

Fish
Lake fish is plentiful and served in multiple ways. As an *antipasto*, it may come marinated, smoked, soused or puréed, as a *primo* it is added to pasta and risottos, and as a *secondo* it may be stuffed with vegetables and herbs, cooked in a sauce, or just grilled, fried or baked.

The most common species are *lavarello*, a white lake fish, perch *(persico)*, trout *(trota)*, pike *(luccio)* and char *(salmerino)*. Lake Iseo's speciality is *tinca ripiena*, baked tench stuffed with breadcrumbs, Parmesan and parsley and served with polenta. Around lakes Iseo and Como, menus may feature *missultini (or missultitt)*; this is twaite shad, which has been stretched out on racks to dry in the sun, then grilled and served with olive oil and vinegar. On Lake Garda look out for the highly prized *carpione*, a type of carp, and *coregone*

in crosta, a white fish flavoured with fennel and cooked in a salt crust.

Meat
Although fish is king around the lakes, most menus also offer a range of meat dishes. Along with simply cooked steak, pork, chicken or veal, you will find dishes of more humble origin: braised donkey, stewed tripe or, on the Padua plain, frogs' legs, eels and snails. The main Milanese specialities are *osso buco* (veal shank stew), *cotoletta alla milanese* (veal cutlet fried in breadcrumbs) and *cassoeula* (pork and cabbage casserole). Game features in the mountains, and in Trentino you will find Austrian-style sausages and sauerkraut, smoked hams and *speck*.

Cheese
The region excels in delicious cheeses, from tangy gorgonzola and pungent taleggio to creamy stracchino, robiola and mascarpone. Parmesan-like Grana Padano, produced on the Padua plain, can be eaten sliced as an appetiser or part of a cheese platter, and is used in many pasta and risotto recipes. Market stalls have dozens of regional cheeses, marked *freschi* (fresh) or *stagionati* (mature). If in doubt, sample a cheese or two before buying.

WHAT TO DRINK

Wine and liqueurs
The DOC *(denominazione di origine controllata)* is an official mark of quality, but

Lake fish drying in the sun   *Romantic dinner in Sirmione*

don't ignore the *vino da tavola* (house wine), which is often a good local wine. In more sophisticated establishments you will be handed a hefty tome of wines, predominantly regional and national, but international too. Neighbouring Piedmont, Emilia-Romagna and the Veneto, all of which produce larger quantities of wine than Lombardy, will feature on most wine lists.

Although not one of Italy's great wine-producing regions, Lombardy has over a dozen wine-producing areas, and a quarter of the wine is DOC. The best of the red wine is produced on the steep slopes of the Valtellina in northern Lombardy: Grumello, Inferno, Sassella and Valgella. Franciacorta, south of Lake Iseo, is best known for sparkling spumante, made from Pinot and Chardonnay grapes. This is often drunk with fish in local restaurants as well as an *aperitivo*. From the shores of Lake Garda come the white Custoza and Lugana, the red Garda Valtenesi and the light, scented red and rosé Bardolinos.

A good meal is usually concluded with a *digestivo* (liqueur), such as a brandy, grappa or limoncello (made from lemons).

Coffee

If you want a small black coffee, ask for a *caffè*, or for a milky coffee, a *caffè latte* (ask for a 'latte' and you will probably get a glass of milk). This and *cappuccino* (or *cappuccio* as the locals call it) are only drunk at breakfast in Italy, although Italians are used to tourists asking for it at all times of day. A good halfway house is a *caffè macchiato*, an espresso with a dash of frothy milk in a small cup. If you want something with a real kick, order a *caffè doppio*, a double espresso; or after a meal, try a *caffè corretto*, with grappa, brandy or Sambuca added. For a good night's sleep forget the real thing and order a *caffè decaffeinato* or *decaff*.

Dessert

Dessert *(dolce)* is typically an almond or apple tart, or a cake, especially *tiramisù*, the alcoholic chocolate and coffee gateau. You may prefer to do as the Italians and buy an ice cream from the local *gelateria*, enjoying it while strolling down the street. After all, the Italians are said to make the best ice cream in the world.

Vegetarians

Although Italy lags behind the UK in its choice of vegetarian dishes, there is an increasing number of restaurants offering at least one meat-and-fish-free dish. Where there are no main vegetarian dishes on offer, opt for a vegetable-based *antipasto* and *primo* (first course), but check first that stocks used for sauces are meat-free. Fresh, seasonal vegetables, often used to enrich pasta and risotto dishes, include *melanzane* (aubergines/eggplant), *carciofi* (artichokes), *zucchini* (courgettes), *radicchio* (red-leaved chicory), *funghi* (mushrooms) and *porcini* (wild boletus mushrooms).

Shopping street in Bellagio

SHOPPING

The fact that most Italians now use the expression 'fare lo shopping' may suggest a globalisation of the shopping scene. But the advent of shopping malls has barely dented the popularity of boutiques, gourmet food shops and markets.

Style and elegance are reflected in the chic stores of Milan, one of the world's fashion powerhouses, and, to a lesser extent, in smaller cities such as Brescia, Como ('City of Silk') and Bergamo. The lakeside towns and villages offer less choice and higher prices, but an altogether more relaxed shopping experience.

FOOD AND DRINK

Small food shops throughout the lakes region display a wide variety of tempting delicacies, from home-cured hams and handmade pastas to herbs and honey to local wines and liqueurs. Milan's temple of deli gastronomy is legendary Peck (Via Spadari 9; www.peck.it), a stunning showcase of cheeses, hams, truffles and foie gras. The shores of Lake Garda offer home-spun aromatic olive oil, Bardolino wines and Limoncello liqueur made from locally grown lemons, while the winegrowing Franciacorta region produces the best fizz in Italy.

MARKETS

Weekly markets are colourful open-air affairs, with stalls selling flowers, food, fashions, household goods and more. Every Wednesday Luino on Lake Maggiore hosts what it claims to be the biggest weekly market in Europe (350 or so stalls), with bargain-hunters descending from Switzerland, Austria and Germany as well as Italy. Monthly antiques markets are a source of local handicrafts, although real bargains are rare. Nevertheless, bargaining, even if only in sign language, is always worth a try.

FASHION IN MILAN

Since the 1980s Milan has been a world centre for fashion design, drawing huge numbers of visitors – many celebrities among them – to the fashion fairs and the flagship stores of Armani, Prada and other top designers. At the opening of the fairs, the international paparazzi descend on the city, while the hip hotels and stylish restaurants are packed with celebrities and supermodels.

The flagship outlets of the big designer names are conveniently concentrated in a small, attractive area, known as the Quadrilatero d'Oro (Golden Quadrangle). Stores range from chic little boutiques to modern emporia

Silk ties from Como

Shoe shop in Salò

such as Armani, complete with restaurant, bookstore, flower shop and furnishings, as well as fashions.

Prices are not for the faint-hearted, but if your credit card can't stretch to cutting-edge collections, there are plenty of more affordable fashions in the city centre, as well as the arty and ethnic boutiques of the Brera and Ticinese quarters.

COMO SILK

Como, centre of Italy's silk industry, has produced silk and other textiles since the 15th century. Silkworms are no long longer bred here, but Chinese fibres are imported to be woven, dyed, designed and printed. Top designers still depend on Como for their silk but the industry has been in steady decline over the past decades, with competition from China, and increasingly high prices of silk as Chinese farmers turn to more lucrative crops. Como shops no longer dazzle with Como silk but you can still find ties and scarves – and a museum (see page 12) that documents the story of this fascinating industry.

Factory outlets

The lakes region has a number of *spacci* (discount factory outlets), selling seductive clothes, cult-design icons, crafts, leatherware and gourmet gifts. One of the few surviving silk outlets around Como is Frey Emporio della Seta in Fino Mornasco (Via Risorgimento 49; www.frey.

it), southwest of Como which sells hand-painted silk scarves, shirts and ties of top designers at 30 to 50 percent discount. At the Foxtown Outlet (www.foxtown.ch) in the Swiss village of Mendrisio 15km (6 miles) northeast of Como you can snap up brands such as Gucci, Verace, Dolce & Gabbana and Prada. Silk manufacturer Mantero – supplier to Yves Saint Laurent, Calvin Klein and other big names – have a small shop here. The functional but well-designed Franciacorta Outlet Village (Rodengo Saiano, 7km/4.5 miles west of Brescia; (www.franciacortaoutlet.it) has over 160 stores. Armani fans should head for its outlet at Vertemate, south of Como, which has some great bargains in its three-storeyed warehouse.

BERGAMO AND BRESCIA

In the heart of the region, Bergamo is a delightful city for shopping as well as sightseeing. The choice is not huge, but the upper town has some lovely food shops and clothes boutiques, while Il Sentierone and Via XX Settembre in the lower town have fashions, silk, leather goods and jewellery. A shuttle bus service links the upper and lower towns with the airport just 5km (3 miles) away which is opposite the huge Orio shopping centre (www.oriocenter.it). The town of Brescia has plenty of classy boutiques with designer fashions, bags and shoes. For the chic shops head for Corso Palestro, Corso Zanardelli, Via Gramsci and Via X Giornate.

Classic–car rally in the lakes

ENTERTAINMENT

The lakeside towns tend to be peaceful places by night, favouring leisurely dinners, lakeside strolls and a liqueur at a local bar. But entertainment is never far away, whether in the clubs of Brescia and Bergamo, at the opera or in Milan's hip bars.

The Lombardy region has a strong musical tradition. Violinmaker Stradivarius and composer Monteverdi both came from Cremona, Donizetti was born and died in Bergamo, and Verdi composed *La Traviata* while staying on Lake Como. Today opera, concerts and music festivals take place in cities across the region and in castles, villas and other historic locations around the lakes.

Opera in Verona

If you are staying on the south or east side of Lake Garda, try to take in an opera extravaganza in nearby Verona's great Roman amphitheatre. The experience is an unforgettable one, and you don't have to be an opera buff to enjoy it. The lavish, open-air performances take place from mid-June to the beginning of September, and the operas alternate, so that in one month you have a choice of three or four different performances. Book well in advance on www.arena.it or tel: 045-800 5151 (tickets range enormously, from €24 to around €220).

FESTIVALS AND EVENTS

The lakes and Lombard cities stage some of the finest events on the Italian cultural calendar. Events take place all year round, and include classical music festivals, boat processions, food and wine fairs, fireworks over the lake and jazz extravaganzas.

The most prestigious event of the lakes is Stresa's Settimane Musicali (www.stresafestival.eu), a July through September festival of classical concerts with internationally renowned musicians, performed in churches and other historical venues by Lake Maggiore.

Brescia plays host to a piano festival from April through June, and the Mille Miglia vintage car race in May. Gardone Riviera on Lake Garda presents drama, opera and concerts in the open-air theatre of the Vittoriale degli Italiani in July and August, while Riva del Garda hosts a two-week musical festival in late July.

The tiny wine-producing region of Franciacorta south of Lake Iseo stages a sparkling wine and food festival in September, along with wine- and food-tasting events in the vineyards at weekends (www.stradadelfranciacorta.

La Scala   *Salò by night*

it). The Grape and Wine Festival at Bardolino (famed for its red wine) on Lake Garda is another cork-popping event held in the autumn. This is the time to buy quantities of wine very cheaply.

Festival of San Giovanni

One of the most ancient and magical lake festivals is that of San Giovanni (St John), celebrated at Isola Comacina, Lake Como, on the weekend closest to St John the Baptist's Day (24 June). Mass is held in the church ruins, and thousands of bobbing boats are illuminated by candles and fireworks. For some of the best views, you can join a night cruise with onboard dinner and dancing (see www.navigazionelaghi.it for details).

Angera's Rocca Borromeo is one of the many venues of the Settimane Musicale di Stresa (www.stresafestival.eu), the top classical music festival of the region. Founded in 1961, it has expanded from Stresa to towns and villages all around Lake Maggiore.

From spring to late summer concerts take place in churches and historic buildings, and on islands. Another venue is the lovely hermitage of Santa Caterina del Sasso (see page 39). Events feature the festival's own resident orchestra, as well as renowned international musicians.

NIGHTLIFE

Milan apart, the region is not really renowned for discos and nightclubs.

Garda is the liveliest of the lakes, particularly in the town of Desenzano del Garda, where bars, live music and nightclubs attract a younger crowd.

Como, although not exactly a hot spot, has some sociable late-opening bars along the Lungo Lario Trieste waterfront.

Brescia tends to get quite lively after dark, especially at the weekends. You can enjoy concerts and opera at the Teatro Grande, or live it up at late-night bars or discos.

Bergamo offers upmarket wining and dining, classical concerts and plenty of bars, but for nightclubs you need to head out of town.

Milan

Milan offers some of the most vibrant nightlife in Italy, with a huge range of classical concerts, theatre, live jazz and rock, pop concerts and scores of stylish *aperitivo* bars and nightclubs. It is also home to La Scala (tel: 02-88791; www.teatroallascala.org), one of the world's most prestigious opera houses (see page 100). If you want to attend a performance, it's advisable (and often essential) to book well in advance.

To find details of clubs, pubs and trendsetting cocktail bars in Milan check out the excellent website www.ciaomilano.it. Another useful source of information is *Hello Milano* magazine (www.hellomilano.it), an online guide to what's on in the city.

Lake Garda sailing

ACTIVITIES

Lake Garda is a sporting paradise, boasting windsurfing, sailing, hiking and cycling, while at Ascona on Lake Maggiore you can ski in the morning and then play a round of golf in the afternoon.

WATERSPORTS

Lake Garda has countless sailing regattas, including world championships. Riva del Garda and Torbole have numerous watersports schools with gear to rent and tuition for all levels. On Lake Maggiore, Laveno, Luino, Ascona and Locarno are bases for sailing and windsurfing. On Lake Como the town of Como offers sailing, water-skiing, diving and canoeing, while further up the lake at Menaggio and Bellagio you can water-ski and hire motorboats, canoes or kayaks. Lakeside lidos and pebbly 'beaches' are popular in high season. Bellagio's revamped lido comes with beach bathing area, sunbeds, cocktail bar and nightlife.

HIKING AND CLIMBING

Ridges above the lakes, woodland trails and the Alpine mountains provide wonderful scenery and cater for all levels of hiking fitness. At Torbole and Riva del Garda freeclimbers hang above the lake, and Arco, further north, has hosted international climbing and paraclimbing championships.

On Lake Garda the Monte Baldo ridge has clear trails and fine views, as does Monte Mottarone above Lake Maggiore. Both have cable car access (from Stresa and Malcesine respectively).

For hikes in the Alps, the best months are May to October. The Club Alpino Italiano or CAI (Italian Alpine Club; www.cai.it) organises guided tours, provides maps and runs shelters for hikers. Many of the routes are not as well marked or developed as in other European countries, and for serious hiking you may want to hire one of their local guides.

CYCLING AND MOUNTAIN BIKING

Lombardy alone has nearly 700 cycling clubs and 1,200 annual races. Every May 20,000 bikers descend on Riva del Garda for the Sympatex Bike Festival, with exhibitions, shows, competitions and stunts. The steep slopes around the lakes are popular with mountain bikers, and the Riva del Garda bike festival in spring attracts top cycling celebrities. For a thrilling ride down a mountain without the uphill struggle, take a bike on the cable

Cycling is a true passion here

car up to Monte Baldo or Monte Mottarone – or hire one at the top.

The steep hill of the Madonna del Ghisallo (12km/7.5 miles south of Bellagio) serves as a challenging last lap of a number of national and local cycling races. Thousands of cyclists and visitors come here annually – and not just for the panoramic views of Lake Como. At the top of the hill is a church dedicated to the Madonna del Ghisallo, who in 1949 was declared the patroness of cyclists by official papal edict. The church then became a cycling museum, displaying bikes and equipment of cycling champions, historic models, trophies and other memorabilia. The state-of-the-art three-storey Museo del Ciclismo (Cycling Museum; www. museodelghisallo.it) beside the church houses some of the exhibits.

GOLF

Lakes Maggiore, Como and Garda have golf courses, many with wonderful views. Some of the finest are around Franciacorta and Lake Garda: the Franciacorta Golf Club (www.franciacortagolfclub.it) is to the south of Lake Iseo, while Bogliaco Golf Resort (www. golfbogliaco.com) and Garda Golf (www. gardagolf.it) are both to the west of Lake Garda between Salò and Desenzano del Garda. The oldest club is the Menaggio and Cadennabia Golf Club (www.menaggio.it) at Lake Como, which was set up by four Englishmen over 110 years ago. Another prestigious location is the Villa d'Este Golf Club (www.villadeste.com).

EXTREME SPORTS

Paragliding is popular on Monte Baldo, Monte Maddalena near Brescia, and from Malcesine (Tandem Flights; www. paraglidingmalcesine.com). Lake Garda's winds are ideal for kitesurfing. The Stickl Sportcamp organises courses for all levels, communicating with kitesurfers through radio receivers fitted into the helmets. If you wish to leap head first down a ravine, try bungee jumping at Verzasca (220m/720ft) and Centovalli (70m/220ft) in Swiss Ticino.

ROCK-CLIMBING

The northern end of Lake Garda, where walls rise to 1,200m (3,900ft), is a haven for rock-climbers. Arco, just north of Torbole, has Europe's largest open-air wall and hosts the Rock Master free-climbing world championships in September.

SKIING

For guaranteed snow you have to head as far north as Bormio. Snow permitting, you can also ski and snowboard at Monte Baldo on Lake Garda, Monte Mottarone and Macugnaga on Lake Maggiore, the Grigna mountains above Lecco on Lake Como, and the resorts above Bergamo and Brescia.

Battle of Solferino in 1859

HISTORY: KEY DATES

The lakes' proximity to the great trade routes between the Mediterranean and Central Europe ensured prosperity and enticed foreign invasion. Each new arrival made its mark, contributing a rich history and culture to this fine region.

EARLY HISTORY

8,000BC   Emergence of the Valle Camonica civilisation, with the first rocks carved by Camuni tribes.

202–191BC   Romans start to establish colonies in Milan, Como, Brescia, Verona and other settlements.

222BC   Romans conquer Milan.

AD313   Emperor Constantine grants freedom of worship to Christians in the Edict of Milan.

4th century   Milan becomes the de facto capital of the western Roman Empire.

568   The Lombards establish their capital at Pavia.

THE MIDDLE AGES

774   Charlemagne takes the Lombard crown.

1024   Emergence of the comuni, or independent city states.

1118–27   Como defeated by Milan in the Ten Years War.

1152   The German prince Frederick Barbarossa is named as the Holy Roman Emperor.

1260–1387   Lake Garda and Verona ruled by Scaligeri (della Scala) dynasty.

1277–1447   Duchy of Milan ruled by the Visconti dynasty.

1347–8   The Black Death devastates the population of northern Italy.

1405   Venetians conquer Verona, Padua and Bergamo.

1450–99   Duchy of Milan ruled by the Sforza dynasty.

FOREIGN INTERVENTION

1530   Charles V is crowned as the Holy Roman Emperor, and Lombardy consequently comes under his rule.

1714   Spain cedes Lombardy to the Austrian (Habsburg) empire.

1796   Napoleon invades northern Italy.

A steamer on Lake Como

1814–70 The Risorigmento – a movement for the liberation and political unification of Italy.

1848 The Milanese rebel against the Austrians, who re-enter the city.

1859 France defeats Austria at the battles of Magenta and Solferino.

1861 Italy is unified under Vittorio Emanuele II, first king of Italy.

1871 Italian unification.

20TH CENTURY

1915 Italy joins the World War I Allies.

1922 Mussolini seizes power in Italy.

1940 Italy enters World War II as an ally of Nazi Germany.

1943–5 Italy surrenders to the Allies; Mussolini is installed in the Republic of Salò.

1945 Mussolini and his mistress, Claretta Petacci, are captured by partisans and executed.

1951 Italy joins the EEC, forerunner of the European Union (EU).

1992 Tangentopoli ('Bribesville') corruption scandals rock the north and lead to an overhaul of public life.

21ST CENTURY

2001 Silvio Berlusconi is elected prime minister.

2002 The euro replaces the lira as the official Italian currency.

2008 Berlusconi starts his fourth term as Prime Minister.

2010 Milan chosen to host EXPO 2015.

2011 Mario Monti brought in as PM to rescue Italy from the debt crisis.

2013 Pope Benedict XVI resigns and is succeeded by Pope Francis I.

2013 The anti-establishment Five Star Movement, co-founded by ex-comedian Beppe Brillo, stunned the mainstream parties when it took a quarter of the votes in the general election.

2015 President Giorgio Napolitano resigns and is succeeded by Sergio Mattarella.

2016 A series of severe earthquakes occurred in Central Italy causing extensive damage, injuries and deaths.

2017 Italy fails to qualify for the 2018 FIFA World Cup, the first time since 1958.

2018 Ponte Morandi viaduct collapses in Genoa killing 43 people.

2019 France recalls its Italian ambassador following a diplomatic incident.

2020 Rome will be one of 12 cities to host the 2020 UEFA European Championship.

BEST ROUTES

Isola Bella

THE BORROMEAN ISLANDS

An island-hopping day trip from the belle époque resort of Stresa to Isola Bella, Isola dei Pescatori and Isola Madre at the centre of Lake Maggiore. Explore the villas and grounds of these three small exotic outcrops, lunching in a rustic fish restaurant on Isola dei Pescatori.

DISTANCE: 13km (8 miles) return trip by ferry
TIME: A full day
START/END: Stresa
POINTS TO NOTE: Regular ferries operate from Stresa to the islands. Pick up a timetable from the ferry station or check times on www.navigazionelaghi. it. If you do not want the restrictions of a timetable, consider taking one of the not-too-extortionate private boats by the ferry station. The ferry service stops in the early evening, but if you wish to dine on the Isola dei Pescatori, both the Verbano and Belvedere restaurants offer a free boat service. Reserve a table for lunch or dinner. The islands are packed throughout the season; make an early start if you want to see all three islands in a day and avoid the worst of the crowds.

Located off the shore of Stresa (see page 34), the Borromean Islands lie at the centre of Lake Maggiore, which, despite its name, is the second-largest Italian lake after Garda. The long, narrow ribbon of water stretches 65km (40 miles) and is bordered by Lombardy to the east, Piedmont to the west and the Swiss canton of Ticino to the north. The scenery varies from the wild northern mountainous, where the Swiss pre-Alps descend towards the lake, to the gentler Mediterranean-like shores of the south.

ISOLA BELLA

At the ferry station on Piazza Marconi, beside the tourist office, buy a ticket that includes entrances to the island sights. Alight at the first stop – Isola Bella.

Whereas Isola dei Pescatori was styled as a rural retreat and Isola Madre as an enchanted garden, **Isola Bella ❶** (www.borromeoturismo.it; mid-Mar– mid-Oct daily 9am–5.30pm; charge) was always intended to be a showy pleasure palace. In recent times Isola Bella has served as the Borromean princes' summer residence; the family stays in the island palace. To protect the family's privacy, and its art collection, two-thirds of the palace is closed to the

The view from the Botanical Garden above Stresa

public, but it is still worth seeing, not least for the beguiling Baroque gardens and the palatial treasures on show.

From a rock to a monument

Although Isola Bella began as little more than a rocky islet with a view, over the course of centuries it became a delightful folly. In the 1620s Count Carlo III Borromeo was inspired to create a full-blown monument to his wife Isabella. To realise his vision the rocks were transformed into an island with 10 terraces designed to resemble the prow of a ship in full sail. Boatloads of soil were transported to this barren island, as well as Baroque statuary and the building materials needed for the creation of a palatial villa. The works con-

tinued under his son, Vitiliano VI, and were virtually complete by the time of his death in 1670. Even so, inspired by the original plans, family descendants continued to embellish the island until the 1950s when Vitiliano IX, the last member of the family to attempt major modifications, died before building his cherished harbour.

Borromean Palace

The island creates a dramatic impact as you approach. Disembarking from the ferry, follow the flow to the turreted **Palazzo Borromeo**. The stern façade belies a lavish interior, full of gilt and stucco-work, marble statues and Murano chandeliers. The palace's high-ceilinged rooms contain a fine collection of 16th- to 18th-century northern Italian art, though it is encrusted in a Baroque clutter of stucco-work and heraldic crests, only partially redeemed by bold flourishes such as a cantilevered spiral staircase. Lavishly overstuffed public rooms connect a gilded throne room, an empire-style ballroom and a Flemish long gallery housing tapestries emblazoned with the unicorns that adorn the dynasty's distinctive crest.

Looking out to Lake Maggiore from Isola Bella

The palace has witnessed numerous momentous historical events, and has played host to emperors and statesmen. In 1797 Napoleon slept in one of the bedrooms – a ponderous neoclassical chamber decorated in what was the politically correct Directoire style. The ornate music room was the setting for the Stresa peace conference of 1935: it was here that Italy, Britain and France failed to agree on a strategic response to Hitler's programme of rapid rearmament, a missed opportunity that hastened the momentum towards war.

Grottoes and garden

Designed as a cool summer retreat, the area beneath the palace conceals bizarre artificial **grottoes**, with tufa-stone walls studded with shells, pebbles and fossils. The maritime mood is sustained in the statue of a coolly reclining nude and caverns dotted with marine imagery. This grotesque creation reflects the contemporary taste for *Wunderkammer* – chambers of marvels designed to enchant visitors with their eclectic displays. In the case of Isola Bella, however, the greatest marvel lies outside.

The Baroque **gardens** envelop the palace in sweeping arcs, with dramatic architectural perspectives accentuated by grandiose urns, obelisks, fountains and statues. Although the terraced gardens abound in arbours, water features and statuary, the sum is greater than its parts. Serried ranks of orange and lemon trees meet flower beds before fading into a studied confusion of camellias and magnolias, laurels, cypresses, jasmine and pomegranate.

The ship-shaped **terraces**, crowned by a four-tiered folly studded with shells and topped by cherubs and classical gods, culminate in a huge statue of a heraldic unicorn. It is all rather pompous, but you can't fail to admire the variety of exotic flora, and the sublime views across to Monte Mottarone. The pièce de résistance is a shell-shaped **amphitheatre** that serves as a delightful setting for summer concerts.

After your visit return to the ferry landing stage (the rest of the island is awash with trinket stands and poor-quality tourist restaurants).

ISOLA DEI PESCATORI

A five-minute ferry ride from Isola Bella brings you to **Isola dei Pescatori ➋**, or as you hear the ferrymen announce it, 'Isola Superiore dei Pescatori'. The full name derives from the Latin *superiore*, indicating that it is further north than Isola Bella (Isola Inferiore).

The island is a pretty fishing village less dedicated to fishing than to the preservation of its film-set picturesque appearance. It is a place for pottering down tiny alleys and peering at the lake, or even paddling off the pebble beach facing Isola Bella. The maze of passageways conjures up the mood of a remote Greek island. Henry James praised this

The Baroque gardens of Palazzo Borromeo

pocket of Italy for making one feel 'out of the rush and crush of the modern world'.

Lunch break

Of the three islands the Isola dei Pescatori is the best bet for lunch, with two inviting waterside restaurants serving fresh fish: the **Hotel Ristorante Verbano**, see ❶, adjoining the pebble beach, or the **Hotel Ristorante Belvedere**, see ❷, five minutes' walk north.

After lunch take the next ferry to Isola Madre, which stops at the resort of Baveno en route.

ISOLA MADRE

Enjoy the cooling breezes on the ferry to **Isola Madre** ❸ (www.borromeoturismo.it; Mar–Oct daily 9am–5.30pm; charge). Here on the largest of the islands, and what was once the wildest, you will find gently landscaped gardens. The island is home to Europe's largest Kashmiri cypress and some of the first camellias planted in Italy. Best seen in spring, the camellias are part of a patchwork formed by shady paths, ancient cedars, mimosa, magnolias and giant rhododendrons, and populated by white peacocks, Chinese pheasants and parrots. The best time to visit is April for camellias or May for azaleas and rhododendrons. In 2006 a freak storm uprooted the island's great Kashmiri Cypress tree. A huge rescue effort, involving cranes brought over by helicopter and ropes to secure it,

seems to have paid off, and new growth is now showing.

The 16th-century **villa** – an apparently austere Mannerist affair created as a home rather than a palace – is a bit stifling and gloomy. The Borromean family indulged their love of theatre here – check out the curious collection of puppet theatres, puppets and dolls.

In the evening you could also dine on Isola dei Pescatori – it is at its most romantic when the crowds have gone. Otherwise, return to Stresa, bearing in mind the last ferry departs at around 6.30pm.

Food and Drink

❶ HOTEL RISTORANTE VERBANO

Via Ugo Ara 2, Isola dei Pescatori; tel: 0323-30408; http://www.hotelverbano.it/; €€

An atmospheric restaurant with a lakeside terrace overlooking Isola Bella that is especially fine in the evenings. Fish-based cuisine. Free evening boat service from/to Stresa.

❷ HOTEL RISTORANTE BELVEDERE

Via di Mezzo, Isola dei Pescatori; tel: 0323-32292; www.belvedere-isolapescatori.it; €

An idyllic waterside setting with meals served in the garden, on the veranda or in the lakeview dining room. The emphasis is on lake fish. Free evening boat service from/to Stresa.

The view of the lake from the Stresa rooftops

STRESA AND ANGERA CASTLE

This tour combines a stroll in Stresa, 'Queen of the Lake', with a cruise of the southern section of Lake Maggiore, alighting at Angera for a leisurely fish lunch and the finest fortress on the lake.

DISTANCE: Walk in Stresa: 3km (2 miles); cruise to Angera and back: 32km (20 miles)
TIME: A half day or leisurely full day
START/END: Stresa
POINTS TO NOTE: Check ferry times at least a day in advance from the landing stage at Piazza Marconi or from the tourist office next door (tel: 0323-30150). Timetables are also available online at www.navigazionelaghi. it. Boats from Stresa to Angera are spasmodic, but there is always a late-morning ferry (50 mins) and a hydrofoil (20 mins but more expensive). The last boats back from Angera leave mid-afternoon. Note that both recommended restaurants in Angera close on Mondays.

STRESA

The main resort on the Piedmontese shore, **Stresa** ❶ was a *belle époque* wintering ground, the popularity of which was enhanced by the opening of the Simplon Pass in 1906. This allowed a railway from the other side of the Alps, giving Stresa instant access.

A dowager resort distinctly past its prime, Stresa is considered to be the noble part of Lake Maggiore. It found favour with both Queen Victoria and Winston Churchill, and remains popular with superannuated politicians and former world leaders. It may have lost the cachet it once enjoyed, but as a base on the lake the resort still can't be beaten for views, excursions and easy access to the Borromean Islands.

Lakeside promenade

From Stresa's bustling waterfront at Piazza Marconi take the **lakeside promenade** northwest towards the sandy Lido and Monte Mottarone cable-car. The main road divides the garden-lined promenade from the succession of imposing hotels and elegant villas. Replete with beguiling vistas over the Borromean Islands, the lakeside rose gardens have a sedate air that complements the resort's genteel reputation.

Angling at dusk

The 15-minute stroll towards Baveno passes Stresa's grandest hotels, the sole relic of its *fin de siècle* heyday. The 18th-century **Villa Ducale**, where the philosopher Antonio Rosmini died in 1855 (and which is now the Rosmini Study Centre) gives way to the Art Nouveau Regina Palace and its renowned restaurant, followed by the **Grand Hôtel des Iles Borromées**, where literary luminaries have stayed (see page 105). Among them was Ernest Hemingway, who recuperated here after being wounded in battle and then used the resort as a backdrop in *A Farewell to Arms* (1929). At the end of the promenade you come to the Lido and a cable-car which rises up to Monte Mottarone for superb lake views (see page 38).

CRUISE TO ANGERA

Retrace your steps to the landing stage for a ferry to Angera and secure a seat on the right of the boat. The route hugs the western shore before crossing to the Lombardy side of the lake.

During the cruise you will pass Stresa's neoclassical **Villa Pallavicino**, with landscaped grounds and an appealing zoo, and the delightful village of **Belgirate**. Further south, towards Arona, are clusters of celebrity villas, especially around **Meina**.

ANGERA AND ROCCA BORROMEO

In **Angera** the medieval hulk of the **Rocca Borromeo** ❷ (Via alla Rocca; www.isoleborromee.it; mid-Mar–3rd week Oct 9am–5.30pm; charge), dominating the town, soon looms into view. In the 11th century the twin fortresses of Arona and Angera were built to safeguard the strategic southern part of the lake. Arona's fortress was destroyed by Napoleon. Angera's, the best-preserved castle on the lake, became the property of the Milanese

The Rocca Borromeo's imposing walls

Visconti in the late 13th century, but in 1450 it passed to the Borromean dynasty, who converted it into a residence and have owned it ever since. The Visconti covered the walls with frescoes celebrating the glory and longevity of their dynasty. The Gothic **Sala di Giustizia** (Hall of Justice), a vaulted chamber, is adorned with signs of the zodiac and scenes of military victories. For fine views over the lake take the rickety steps up the **Torre Principale**.

Doll Museum

A dozen rooms of the castle are devoted to the **Museo della Bambola**, one of the largest collections of dolls in Europe. Dating from the 18th to the 20th century, the dolls are remarkably detailed and varied; they are made of everything from wood and wax to papier mâché, fabric and plastic. The collection also features dolls' furniture, toys, board games and children's clothes from the 18th century, plus fully functioning late 19th- and early 20th-century French and German automatons (1870–1920).

Lunch with a view

For lunch the best options are the restaurant of the **Vecchia Angera** in the Hotel Pavone, see ❶, a 10–15-minute walk south from the Rocca Borromeo, or the lakeside **Hotel Lido**, see ❷.

This is the narrowest section of Lake Maggiore and, mists permitting, there should be good views across to **Arona** on the Piedmontese shore. Towering over the town is the **San Carlone** – a colossal statue of the locally born, beatified reformer San Carlo Borromeo (1538–84) – which, when built, was the world's tallest statue after New York's Statue of Liberty.

San Carlone

The Rocca Borromeo, like the Borromean Islands off Stresa, belongs to the Borromeo dynasty. A famous member of the family was San Carlo (St Charles), who was born in 1538 in the (now-ruined) castle of Arona and devoted his life to the reform and welfare of the Church. A meteoric rise to power saw him become a cardinal at the age of 22 and archbishop of Milan at 26. Carlo founded seminaries and religious colleges, and worked ceaselessly during the plague of 1576–8, accommodating the sick, burying the dead and risking his own health in doing so. He was canonised posthumously by Pope Paul V in 1610. A huge statue of the saint, familiarly known as San Carlone (big St Charles), stands above Arona. You can climb right up inside the statue and look through his eyes – though it is stifling to do so on a hot summer's day. After a ten-year closure the grounds of the castle have reopened to the public.

Exterior view of Rocca Borromeo

BACK TO STRESA

After lunch take the ferry or hydrofoil back to Stresa. On arrival you might want to regain your land legs before going to your hotel or embarking on a dinner cruise. The resort is short of specific sights, but it does possess a certain faded charm, from a tiny harbour full of fishing boats to bustling **Piazza Cadorna**, the main inland square. Sit down under the plane trees and sip a drink in **Caffè Nazionale** or get an ice cream at the nearby **Angolo del Gelato**.

This is prime shopping time, so you could saunter down Via Bolognaro to see the old-fashioned shops, or continue to Via Garibaldi, parallel with the lakeshore, which has a reliable pastry shop-Pasticceria Caffetteria Bravi at No. 6. If planning a picnic for the following day, call in at Stresa's main supermarket, Carrefour, located at Via Roma 11, just off Piazza Cadorna.

For dinner avoid the restaurants on Piazza Cadorna in favour of **La Botte**, see ❸, or **La Piemontese**, see ❹, both on Via Mazzini, the street linking Piazza Cadorna and Piazza Matteotti.

Food and Drink

❶ LA VECCHIA ANGERA

Hotel Pavone, Via F. Borromeo 14, Angera; tel: 0331-930 224; www.hotelpavone. it; €€

An unpretentious restaurant patronised by locals as well as tourists. The choice of fish depends on availability from the market; the pastas and puddings are all home-made. Typical dishes are tagliatelle with squid and Pachino tomatoes, risotto with *porcini* and Parmesan, and sea bass baked in a salt crust.

❷ HOTEL LIDO

Viale Libertà 11, Angera; tel: 0331-930 232; www.hotellido.it; Tue–Sun; €€

A good fish restaurant within a lakeshore hotel. Try the tagliolini with lemon and burrata with sea algae and red prawns, and

the cod steak with artichoke cream, or lakefish sushi, and select from 300 wines.

❸ LA BOTTE

Via Mazzini 6/8, Stresa; tel: 0323-30462; Thu–Tue €

'The Barrel' is a tiny wood-panelled, ambient, chef-owned restaurant in a narrow street a minute's walk from the main piazza. Dishes include seasonal specialities, local sausages, and good pastas and pizzas.

❹ LA PIEMONTESE

Via Mazzini 25, Stresa; tel: 0323-30235; Tue–Sun; www.ristorantepiemontese.com; €€€

A long-established Stresa restaurant with a delightful setting and friendly atmosphere. Meals are taken in the cosy dark-wood interior or the vine-covered terrace. Great lake fish, wonderful cheeses, heavenly desserts and choice vintage wines.

The view from Santa Caterina del Sasso

MONTE MOTTARONE AND SANTA CATERINA

Climb by cable-car to the Monte Mottarone peak, a natural balcony that overlooks the Alps and lakes; then take a ferry to Santa Caterina del Sasso, an enchanting medieval hermitage that clings to a cliff by Lake Maggiore.

DISTANCE: Walking: 1.5km (1 mile); ferry return trip 9km (5.5 miles)
TIME: A full day
START/END: Stresa
POINTS TO NOTE: Choose a clear day for Monte Mottarone and take something warm to wear. Check out afternoon ferry times to and from Santa Caterina (there is at least one an hour) and note the time of the last boat back. There are no midday boats from Stresa, and for a leisurely visit you need to get the earliest afternoon ferry and come back on the penultimate or last boat. There is no café at Santa Caterina, so lunch either on Monte Mottarone or in Stresa, or bring a picnic.

Between lakes Maggiore and Orta, Monte Mottarone (1,491m/4,891ft) commands a magnificent panorama of misty lakes, snow-crested peaks and the Po Valley. On one of the rare clear days the view stretches to seven lakes.

From Piazza Marconi in Stresa it is about a 1.5km (1-mile) walk north-west to the **Monte Mottarone cable-car ❶** (Mar–Oct 9.30am–5.40pm (last descent), every 20 mins; buy tickets at the cable-car; charge).

Access by car

Mottarone can also be reached by car (take the road to Gignese from central Stresa). The last section of the road is owned by the Borromeo family, and you will have to pay a toll.

You can also get to Santa Caterina by car in about an hour. From Stresa drive to Intra (18km/11 miles), then take the Intra–Laveno car ferry (20 mins), and then drive from Laveno to Santa Caterina (5km/3 miles). A short walk from the car park are the 268 steep steps down to the church.

MONTE MOTTARONE

The journey up to Monte Mottarone takes 20 minutes, but it is worth getting out at Alpino, the first stop, to see the rock gardens of the **Giardino Botanico Alpinia** (Alpine Botanical Garden; late Apr–Oct 9.30am–6pm; giardinobotanicoalpinia.

Fresco inside the convent   *Monte Mottarone cable-car*

altervista.org, charge, joint ticket with cable-car available), with over 1,000 species of Alpine and medicinal plants. The latest family attraction is the panoramic Alpyland coaster (www.alpyland. com), where you can ride bobsleighs at speeds of up to 40kph (25mph) come snow or sunshine.

Once at the upper cable-car station, walk for about 15 minutes to get to the **summit ❷** for the best views and **Casa della Neve**, see ❶.

SANTA CATERINA DEL SASSO

Return to Piazza Marconi, where ferries for Santa Caterina leave from the main landing stage. It is only a 15-minute trip, then from the landing stage you have to climb up 80 steps.

The Carmelite convent of **Santa Caterina del Sasso ❸** (summer opening hours from Mar: the Hermitahe daily 9am–7.30pm, church daily 9.30am–5.30pm; www.santacaterinadelsasso.com), seemingly suspended over a rocky precipice and overhung by crags, is at its most romantic when viewed from the lake. Set on the only stretch of Lake Maggiore that has no banks, the hermitage, which is renowned for its Gothic frescoes, guards the deepest parts of the lake. According to legend, it was founded by Alberto Besozzi, a shipwrecked

12th-century moneylender who vowed to become a hermit if he survived.

In 1195 Besozzi's piety was said to have been instrumental in averting a plague, and he was rewarded with the building of a hermitage to the 3rd-century St Catherine of Alexandria. Since 1975 the sanctuary has been entrusted to a small group of lay brothers led by a Benedictine monk.

After your tour of the convent catch the next ferry back to Stresa.

> ## Food and Drink
>
> **❶ CASA DELLA NEVE**
>
> Loc. Mottarone; tel: 0323-763 6962; www. casadellaneve.it; Wed–Mon; €
> This family-run hotel restaurant enjoys great views of the Monte Rosa chain. The peak is snow-capped from December to March, and many of the specialities here are geared to warm up winter skiers: fondues, pork ragout, jugged deer, etc. Lighter fare in summer.

Prized tulips at Villa Taronto

VILLA TARANTO
AND LAKE MERGOZZO

*Take an enjoyable and scenic stroll to Villa Taranto and the most famous gardens
of Lake Maggiore. Walk along Pallanza's fashionable promenade, then discover
tiny Lake Mergozzo and its enchanting fishing village.*

DISTANCE: Ferry: 6km (3.75 miles),
walk: 4km (2.5 miles), bus/taxi: 8km
(5 miles)
TIME: A half day or leisurely full day
START: Stresa
END: Mergozzo
POINTS TO NOTE: Ferries to Villa
Taranto (45 mins) are more direct
but less frequent than those to
Pallanza (about 35 mins and a short
walk to the villa). Allow at least an
hour, but preferably two (or more)
for Villa Taranto. If you want to hire
a bike or take a bus or taxi from
Pallanza to Mergozzo, ask for advice
at Pallanza's tourist office on the
waterfront at Corso Zanitello 6/8 by
Villa Giulia (tel: 0323-503 249), or
call 347 6467370 for a taxi. Buses
are infrequent, but there is a daily
service at around 1pm from Pallanza
(Piazza Gramsci) to Mergozzo (the
Verbania–Domodossola line). A quick
way back to Stresa from Mergozzo via
public transport is a direct train by the
primary train operator Trenitalia (www.
trenitalia.com).

From the jetty on Stresa's Piazza Marconi
take a morning ferry to Villa Taranto (or to
Pallanza, see Points to Note). If you want
to have a picnic lunch, buy provisions
from Supermercato GS at Via Rome 11,
in Stresa, before you leave. (An area near
the entrance of Villa Taranto is allocated
to picnickers; alternatively, you could plan
to picnic on a beach at Lake Mergozzo.)
Most of the boats call en route at **Baveno**, set in the lee of a pink granite mountain. A small, subdued version of Stresa,
the resort prospered from quarried pink
granite and has been popular with British
visitors since Victorian times.

VILLA TARANTO

Pallanza has some fine gardens,
but none of them matches those of
Villa Taranto ❶ (www.villataranto.
it; March 8.30am–5.30pm, Apr–
Sept 8.30am–6.30pm, 1–14 Oct
9am–5pm, 15–31 Oct 9am–4.30pm,
1–3 Nov 9am–4pm; charge). The landing stage, right in front of the entrance,
was created specifically for the gardens
when they opened in 1952.

Giant water lilies   *Perfect symmetry in the gardens*

The garden

In 1931 Neil McEacharn, a retired Scottish soldier and passionate horticulturist, saw an advertisement in *The Times* for the estate known as La Crocetta on a hillside in Pallanza. He bought the property and devoted the rest of his life to planting and landscaping the site. What had formerly been an unruly wooded headland was transformed into one of Europe's leading botanical gardens. McEacharn imported plants from five different continents – most notably from Asia. Among them were exotic plants, such as coffee, tea, cotton, lotus blossom, giant Amazonian water lilies and papyrus.

The gardens have more than 20,000 plant species, and are equally lovely in spring and autumn. Tulip-lined flower beds contrast with exotic aquatic plants; there is also a wooded ravine and a soothing water garden with fountains and ponds. In April and May, cherry blossom floats over violets, narcissi and crocuses, and camellias, azaleas, irises and rhododendrons also all flourish. From 25 April to May every year there are 80,000 bulbs in flower at Villa Taranto. The star is the tulip – over 65 varieties are planted. During the week one ticket out of every five sold at Villa Taranto has a stamp on the back entitling the visitor to a free plant or flower cultivated in the garden.

Summer is the time to see aquatic plants, oleanders, hydrangeas, roses and citrus fruits; autumn for coppery Japanese maples, flowering shrubs and mellow dahlias.

Don't miss the giant water lilies in the Victoria Amazonica Greenhouse. They measure up to 2m (6.5ft), with leaves that look like huge green trays. The flowers, which are nocturnal and pollinated by beetles, only live for around 24 hours, and gradually change colour from creamy white to pink and purplish red.

Since McEacharn left the villa to the state, Villa Taranto has been a venue for political summits (held in the villa itself, which is closed to the public), each marked by a tree-planting ceremony. Trees have been planted here by Margaret Thatcher, Helmut Kohl and Giulio Andreotti.

PALLANZA

Leave the gardens and follow the Via Vittorio Veneto, the lakeside

Colourful Pallanza

road, for about 30 minutes on foot around the headland to Corso Zanitello in **Pallanza** ❷, where magnolia and oleander trees line the quaysides and colourful cafés flank the piazzas.

During the medieval era Pallanza was protected by a castle and was the only town on the lake not to fall under Borromean sway. The resort's mild winter climate, fine views and luxuriant gardens attract the elderly during off-season, while a smattering of bars and clubs in medieval Pallanza draw younger visitors in summer.

Villa Giulia

Just before the tourist office at Nos 6–8 stands the **Villa Giulia**, a frothy pink concoction built in 1847 and originally owned by Bernardino Branca, inventor of Fernet Branca, and now serving as a convention venue. The gardens are a public park and command views of the private islet of San Giovanni, which the conductor Toscanini acquired from the Borromean family.

Eating options

If you are ready for refreshment at this point, the enticing **Ristorante Milano** – called 'glamorous' in a 2017 *New York Times* article – overlooks the picturesque old harbour, see ❶.

Suna

The garden-lined lakeside promenade continues for another 2km (1.25 miles). At the far side of the resort you can watch the watersports around **Suna**. This former fishing village buzzes with beach life, although the occasional villa and Romanesque church hark back to a quieter era. If you are contemplating a meal now or later for dinner, the **Hostaria Dam a Traa**, see ❷, is a friendly restaurant with a terrace overlooking the lake.

Fondotoce Nature Reserve

Towards the end of Via Troubetskoy, the promenade merges into the busy coastal road. The 360ha (890-acre) **Riserva Naturale Fondotoce** protects the wetlands to the west, habitat of numerous species of waterfowl and other marsh bird but the area around Fondotoce is somewhat spoilt by campsites.

LAKE MERGOZZO

By bus or taxi it is about 10km (6 miles) northwest from Pallanza to the village of **Mergozzo** ❸. Framed by forests, tiny **Lago di Mergozzo** is one of

The rooftops of Mergozzo   *Restaurants in Mergozzo*

the cleanest lakes in Europe (motorboats are banned) and the beaches are secluded. Prior to the 9th century it was part of Lake Maggiore, but silt from the River Toce separated it from the larger lake.

Once you arrive at the village of Mergozzo, Ristorante Due Palme, near to the main piazza, is the place from which to see the picturesque hamlet as it curves around the fishing harbour; from here inviting alleys and flights of steps lead to a cloistered church and old-fashioned inns.

For a meal you might opt for delicious pizza, followed by incredible dessert or fancy beer at **Fiore di Latte Pizzeria** see ❸, close to the Hotel Due Palme, which overlooks Lake Mergozzo. Alternatively, sample the tasting menu at **La Quartina**, see ❹, or try the gastronomic delights of Il **Piccolo Lago** (see page 113), but note the opening times.

From Mergozzo catch a bus to Intra/Verbania. Then take the ferry to Stresa.

Food and Drink

❶ RISTORANTE MILANO
Corso Zanitello 2/4, Pallanza; tel: 0323-556 816; www.ristorantemilanolagomaggiore. com; Wed–Mon, closed Tue, may be closed off-season; €€€
Frighteningly pricey, but it is worth splashing out for the romantic lakeside location, the exquisite fish dishes and the succulent meat from Piedmont. Needless to say, the food is freshly sourced, the setting elegant and the service faultless.

❷ HOSTARIA DAM A TRAA
Via Paolo Troubetzkoy 106, Suna; tel: 0323-557152; damatraa.it; closed on Mon; €€-€€€
Wrap yourself in a warm and relaxing atmosphere and discover traditional flavours with an elegant and modern twist. Menu offers typical a la carte dishes as well as dishes of the day. Vegetarian friendly; gluten free options available.

❸ FIORE DI LATTE PIZZERIA
Piazza conte Berrino 6, Mergozzo; tel: 0323 80630; www.fioredilatte.it; Tue–Sun, dinner; €€
Visit this place if you are craving delicious pizza prepared with only the most carefully chosen ingredients. Sit down and enjoy the views of Lake Mergozzo from the terrace.

❹ LA QUARTINA
Hotel La Quartina, Via Pallanza 22, Lago di Mergozzo; tel: 0323-80118; www.laquartina. com; €€
Hugging the shore of Lake Mergozzo, this relaxing hotel-restaurant serves trout from the lake and sea bass, salami, cheese and game from the hills, and a traditional Piedmontese tasting menu.

LAKE MAGGIORE EXPRESS

A combination of lake cruise and mountain railway, crossing from Italy into Switzerland, this tour offers some of the most sensational scenery in Northern Europe. A relaxing three-hour ferry trip is followed by a dramatic narrow-gauge railway ride through the wild Ticino mountains with spectacular views.

DISTANCE: Ferry: 61km (38 miles), train: 96km (60 miles)
TIME: A full day, possibly two
START: Stresa ferry landing stage
END: Stresa railway station
POINTS TO NOTE: Tickets include lake cruise and rail journey. Book in advance, especially in high season. Prices are adult €34, child €17 (two days: adult €44, child €22. Contact Navigazione Lago Maggiore: tel: 800-551 801 (free from Italian phone numbers within Italy); www. lagomaggioreexpress.com. Services operate Mar–Oct, July and Aug daily except Wed, other months Thu–Sun only. Passports are essential. At the Stresa ticket office on Piazza Marconi pick up a ferry timetable and the Lago Maggiore Express leaflet with times of trains from Locarno to Domodossola, and connecting trains from Domodossola back to Stresa. A two-day ticket allows more time to explore the upper lake and mountain villages and includes a free lake pass.

Begin your tour from any ferry stop on Lake Maggiore, taking the cruise north to Locarno in Switzerland.

STRESA TO THE UPPER LAKE

From Stresa, the triple-decker *battello* ferry skirts the **Borromean Islands** and then stops at the resort of **Baveno ❶** (see page 40). The next stop is **Pallanza ❷** (see page 42), where grandiose villas and a garden-lined promenade overlook the lake. From neighbouring Intra, the boat crosses to Laveno on the eastern side of the lake.

UPPER LAKE MAGGIORE

The main resorts of the northern lake lie on the sunny western shores. **Cannero Riviera ❸** occupies a charming site amid subtropical flora, looking over to picturesque islets with ruins of the Malpaga castles. Dating from the 12th century, the castles belonged to the five Mazzarditi brothers, brigands who plundered local villages. The Visconti destroyed their strongholds in 1414,

The train crosses the Swiss border into the canton of Ticino

then a century later the Borromeo family built fortifications here – the remains of which you see today. **Cannobio** ❹, the last town before the Swiss border, has steep medieval streets behind a long promenade of pastel-washed façades. If you are on a two-day ticket, this is definitely a place to explore.

NORTH INTO SWITZERLAND

Across the Swiss border, the first stop is Brissago, which is noticeably more modern than the nearby Italian villages.

The larger of the two **Isole Brissago** ❺ (Brissago Islands) is home to the **Parco Botanico del Cantone Ticino**, created in 1883 by Baroness Antoinette de Saint-Léger and full of exotic flora. She set up residence here and inspired artists, writers and musicians to visit the island.

Ascona

The boat heads on to the little resort of **Ascona** ❻, where multicoloured houses line the waterfront. Paul Klee, Hermann Hesse and Isadora Duncan were among those lured by its charms.

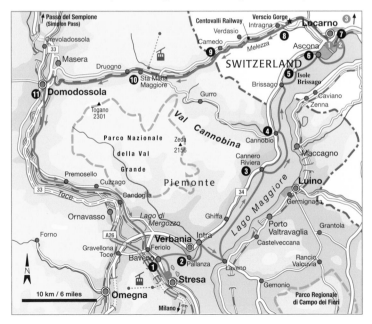

The sanctuary of Madonna del Sasso

LOCARNO

Over the river from Ascona lies **Locarno** ❼, a southwest-facing town with a mild climate and flourishing parks and gardens. Pick up a map when you disembark, or turn left for the tourist office, and locate the nearby station where you will take the train to Domodossola. On a day trip you are likely to have between 1.5–3.5 hours in Locarno, depending on which train you opt for. The 52km (32.5-mile) railway line from Locarno to Domodossola opened in 1923. Until recently passengers travelled in vintage carriages with wooden interiors – more romantic but less comfortable than today's electric trains.

Crossing the border

A fifth of Lake Maggiore lies in Switzerland, in the Italian-speaking canton of Ticino. The resorts are Italian in feel, with their bright piazzas and alfresco eateries, but there is a marked Swiss efficiency about them: while the Italian lakeside villages retain their ancient patina, façades in Switzerland look as though they were painted yesterday. You may be tempted by the stylish shops in Locarno; if so, remember that the local currency is Swiss francs, and although euros are accepted here, you will usually receive change in Swiss francs – often at a poor exchange rate.

The heart of Locarno is the porticoed **Piazza Grande**, just back from the lakefront, where you can sit at cafés and people-watch. In summer this is the venue for open-air concerts, and in August it hosts the International Film Festival. From the piazza follow the lanes running west of the square for the **Città Vecchia** (Old Town) and Via Cittadella, where **La Cittadella**, see ❶, serves excellent pizzas and fish.

Refreshment

You may arrive in Locarno too late to lunch in some of the restaurants, but many cafés and pizzerias open all day. The most inviting spots are Piazza Grande or lakeside Viale Verbano, where **Al Pozz**, see ❷, is open all day for full meals, as is neighbouring **Centenario** (see page 112).

Sanctuary of Madonna del Sasso

For stunning views of the lake and Alps, take the **funicular** (200m/yds northwest of the landing stage; daily starting from around 8am, with the last service in the late afternoon or evening depending on the month; charge) that climbs up the hill every 15 or 30 minutes (depending on the season), or walk up the pathway flanked by chapels to the **Santuario della Madonna del Sasso** (daily 7.30am–6pm), a Capuchin monastery founded in 1480. Here, the **Ristorante Funicolare**, see ❸, is a great spot to admire the view.

CENTOVALLI AND VALLE VIGEZZO

The Centovalli trains depart from below

Sanctuary detail   *Colourful Ascona*

Locarno's **railway station** (Via della Stazione), which is 200m/yds north of the landing stage. Follow directions for Funivia Locarno–Domodossola, and when you board the train secure a seat on the near side for the best views. Once you have emerged from the tunnel, you will be travelling through a wild, spectacular region; the little train snakes its way slowly around steep, wooded valleys, passing waterfalls and crossing precarious-looking bridges and viaducts above dramatic gorges. Deepest of all is the gorge of Verscio, a haven for bungee-jumpers.

Mountain hamlets

The railway follows the course of the River Melezza, stopping at neat mountain hamlets, with their chalet-style houses and lofty steeples. **Intragna** ❽ has a lovely 16th-century bridge, as well as a viaduct (another spot for bungee-jumping. (If you are on the two-day trip, you can take a cable-car up to Costa and Pila from here.)

After a customs-check at **Camedo** ❾ on the border, you are back in Italy. From here, the train climbs up to **Santa Maria Maggiore** ❿, which, at 830m (2,723ft), is the highest point of the journey. The village is home to a several art galleries.

DOMODOSSOLA TO STRESA

The trip ends at **Domodossola** ⓫, not far from the Simplon Pass. From here you should transfer to the normal Trenitalia rail service for Stresa. The final lap of the journey takes just half an hour.

Food and Drink

With advance notice you can be served lunch on board the ferry. This is a simple but adequate three-course meal of pasta, fish or meat and dessert with wine – all for around €20. Alternatively, you can buy a picnic in Stresa and have it on board the boat.

❶ LA CITTADELLA
Via Cittadella 18, Locarno; tel: 00 41-0-91 751 5885; www.cittadella.ch; Tue–Sun; €€
Downstairs is an informal pizzeria, while upstairs is a smart seafood restaurant; the food at both is delicious. Booking advised.

❷ AL POZZ
Viale Verbano 21, Locarno; tel: 00 41-0-91 744 6364; www.alpozz.ch; Wed–Sun; €€
Open all day for pizzas and Mediterranean cuisine, Al Pozz has great views of Lake Maggiore and the mountains from its terrace. *Pollo nel cestello* (chicken in a basket) is a speciality.

❸ RISTORANTE FUNICOLARE
Via Santuario 4, Orselina, Locarno; tel: 00 41-0-91 743 1833; www.ristorantefunicolare.ch; closed Jan–Feb and Thu off-season; €€
Perched above Locarno, at the top of the Sanctuary of Madonna del Sasso, this is worth a trip for the views alone. The menu is likely to feature *filetto di luccio* (pike), as well as meat and pasta. Alternatively, just go for coffee and cake.

Orta San Giulio at dusk

LAKE ORTA

For all its popularity with Italians and foreigners alike, Lake Orta has managed to retain a certain mystique. This driving tour will transport you to a dreamy pocket of Piedmont, the highlights of which are the medieval village of Orta San Giulio and the Isola San Giulio in the centre of the lake.

DISTANCE: 85km (53 miles), returning via Gravellona Toce
TIME: A full day
START/END: Stresa
POINTS TO NOTE: Avoid Orta on Sundays, when coachloads of visitors descend on the village. If you do not have a car, consider booking an organised tour from Stresa through the Orta tourist office (tel: 0322-90155). If you are thinking of a meal at Villa Crespi (see page 114), be sure to reserve.

Separated from Lake Maggiore by the Mottarone peak, Orta is the western-most of the lakes. Just 14km (9 miles) long and 3km (2 miles) wide, it is tiny in comparison to lakes Maggiore, Como or Garda. It is not so much the scenery that makes it unmissable, but the village of Orta San Giulio and the picturesque little Isola San Giulio.

Between lakes Maggiore and Orta, the Mottarone peak commands a wonderful panorama of the lakes and Alps. A road leads up there from Gignese, but be warned: you will have to pay several euros to get there, as the last section is a toll road owned by the omnipotent Borromeo family. You can also access the peak by cable-car from Stresa, or on foot.

GIGNESE

Leaving Stresa by car, follow the signs for Gignese and climb the Mottarone. After 8km (5 miles) you will reach the hill village of **Gignese ❶**, best-known for the **Museo dell'Ombrello e del Parasole** (Umbrella and Parasol Museum; www.gignese.it/museo; Tue–Sun 10am–noon, 3–6pm; charge), a large collection of fanciful umbrellas, dating from 1850. Continue to Armeno and descend southwest towards Lake Orta and Orta San Giulio.

SACRO MONTE

Take the main approach road which passes the entrance to the **Sacro Monte ❷** (Holy Mount; opening times for the church and grounds vary). Leave your car in the higher of the two car parks, which is conveniently situated

Sacro Monte fresco   *Colourful façades, Orta San Giulio*

for access to the pedestrianised historic centre of Orta San Giulio.

Sacri Monti are prominent features of this corner of the lakes, and Orta's is the finest, rivalled only by the one in Varese (see page 53). Linked to tiny chapels, the Sacri Monti are the climax of Franciscan devotional routes that evoke the symbolic journey through the Holy Land. Set on a wooded hillside, Orta's route wends through a series of 20 frescoed chapels, with some 400 life-size terracotta statues that trace the history of St Francis. Slate-roofed Renaissance and Baroque chapels are full of devotional paintings and statues by Lombard artists. The route is well worth following for its peaceful atmosphere and misty views. A stop at **Agrigela-teria** is a great way to start or finish your walk, see ❶.

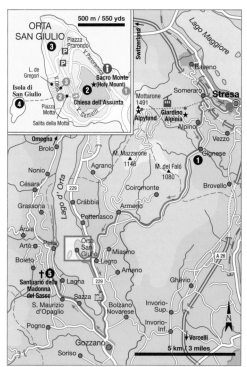

ORTA SAN GIULIO

Set snugly on a peninsula, **Orta San Giulio** ❸ has long been a fashionable if discreet resort, known for its chic hotels as much as for its soft light and air of spirituality. Take the atmospheric Via Gemelli from the Sacro Monte to the village. You will emerge outside the Baroque **Chiesa dell'Assunta** (Church of the Assumption), host of a spring concert festival complete with full historical pageantry. The church commands a dramatic view of the sloping **Salita della Motta**, which winds down to the main square, passing geranium-bedecked balconies and Renaissance palaces with peach-coloured façades.

Piazza Motta

The descent ends at **Piazza Motta** by the quaint waterfront. The piazza is lined with outdoor cafés and old-fashioned hotels, including the **Leon d'Oro**, which has a good restaurant, see ❷. The hub of village life, Piazza Motta is particularly animated during the Wednesday market.

Overlooking the square is the arcaded former town hall, the **Palazzo della Comunità**, frescoes of which feature a serpent symbol relating to Orta's mythical origins. This façade is an exception in the town – buildings here tend to be painted in muted shades of ochre, green or pink; white is forbidden.

Take **Via Olina**, the main thoroughfare, if you want to indulge in some window-shopping in the medieval quarter, and perhaps book a table at the **Olina** restaurant in the Piccolo Hotel, see ❸.

Not far away, on Largo de Gregori, you will find **Salumeria Rovera**, a whimsical salami shop that features somewhat tasteless paintings of piglets tucking into a pork feast.

ISOLA DI SAN GIULIO

At Orta San Giulio's picturesque jetty, friendly boatmen guide ferries and motorboats to the **Isola di San Giulio** ❹, a tiny haven of tranquillity and supplication. In the convent (closed to the public) at the heart of the isle, blue-robed Benedictine nuns devote themselves to contemplation, work and prayer. Note that the village of Orta San Giulio is closed to traffic during the season and cars must be left in the paying parking lots above the centre.

Chattering visitors clambering out of boats beside the **Basilica di San Giulio** (summer 9.30am–12.15pm/2–6pm, winter 9.30am–12.15pm/ 2–7pm) are soon hushed by the sombre mood of this Romanesque church. The island was supposedly overrun by serpents and dragons until AD390, when Julius, a Christian preacher, succeeded in banishing them, before erecting a basilica in celebration. Fragments of the 5th-century church are visible in the crypt.

Spiritual injunctions

The circular **Via Giulino**, which hugs the high walls of the nunnery, carries injunctions to follow the right path. In a bid to evoke 'the island within', there are two pilgrimage paths: the Way of Meditation and the Way of Silence. The island forsakes its silence only in June, when a festival of ancient music is staged.

SANCTUARY OF MADONNA DEL SASSO

After Orta San Giulio, the other towns on the lake come as something of an anticlimax. Nevertheless, if you have time, it is worth taking the short drive to the sanctuary that overlooks the lake.

From Orta San Giulio, head south along the shore towards Gozzano and follow the western shore to San

The magical Isola di San Giulio

Maurizio d'Opaglio, an area known as 'tap country' due to the presence of Italy's finest tap- and bath-makers. While these manufacturers prospered on orders from Arab sheikhs, Lake Orta suffered pollution from industrial waste. However, during the early 1990s a cleaning programme coincided with a collapse of the gold-tap market, resulting in waters fit for swimming once more.

Resist the Tap Museum in San Maurizio d'Opaglio in favour of the **Santuario della Madonna del Sasso** ⑤, which is just 2km (1.25 miles) away, above Pella. Clearly signposted, it is at the heart of a pleasant series of hamlets. The Baroque frescoed church, built on a granite outcrop over the lake, has fine views over mountains and lake.

RETURN TO STRESA

You can return to Lake Maggiore by continuing along the western shore, passing Pella, Nonio and Omegna, then heading north to Gravellona Toce and returning to Stresa via Baveno. Or return the way you came, through Gignese, dining perhaps at Orta San Giulio before heading back to Stresa.

Villa Crespi

If you have a taste for the exotic this is where you will find the **Villa Crespi** (see pages 106 and 114), a fairytale Moorish fantasy erected in 1879 by a local cotton merchant inspired by his travels to Baghdad and Persia. The villa is situated out of the medieval centre, at the entrance to the town, so parking is easy.

Food and Drink

① AGRIGELATERIA
Via Domodossola 5, Orta San Giulio; tel: 339 230 3342; Mon–Fri from 7am, Sat–Sun from 8am; €
A perfect spot to beat the heat either before or after your walk to the Sacro. Kids and adults will enjoy the numerous and delicious flavours. Connected to the ice cream shop is a small pizzeria in case you need a little more sustenance.

② LEON D'ORO
Piazza Motta 42, Orta San Giulio; tel: 0322-911 991; www.albergoleondoro.it; €€
An idyllic location with a long shady terrace overlooking Isola San Giulio and a good-value menu of local dishes, including fresh lake fish and wonderful puddings.

③ OLINA
Via Olina 40, Orta San Giulio; tel: 0322-905656; Thu–Tue; €€
Make the most of the complimentary *aperitivo* and appetiser and tuck into artfully presented local specialities, including vegetarian dishes. Attentive service and some quirky touches.

Sacro Monte di Varese in winter

VARESE AND LAKE LUGANO

A full-day country and lakeside drive from Varese, nudging the Swiss border on Lake Lugano. A tour of Villa Panza's contemporary art collection is followed by a visit to Varese's nature reserve, then lunch in Luino on Lake Maggiore and a scenic drive along the shores of Lake Lugano.

DISTANCE: 85km (53 miles)
TIME: A full day
START/END: Varese
POINTS TO NOTE: Check whether the Campo dei Fiori nature reserve (tel: 0332-435 386) is open before you set out. Note also that unless it is a Sunday or holiday you will need to make an appointment (option only available for groups of 15 or more) to visit Villa Cicogna-Mozzoni (tel: 0332-471 134). Consider making this day trip on a Wednesday, when Luino holds its market (until 5pm); the biggest in the region, it sells food, clothes, leather, textiles, household goods, etc. It is a good idea to bring your passport in case you find yourself seduced by the temptation to visit Switzerland.

VARESE

Begin in the city of **Varese**. Essentially a modern industrial city, Varese has styled itself as a *Città Giardino*, or Garden City. It also has a small historic centre, as well as sophisticated shopping.

Villa Panza

Varese's top cultural attraction is Villa Panza, which houses a major collection of modern American art. From the centre of Varese head north along Via Veratti, which becomes Viale Aguggiari. **Villa Panza** ❶ (www.fondoambiente. it; Tue–Sun 10am–6pm, last entry 45 mins before closing; may be closed on holidays; charge) is signposted to the right after about 1km (0.75 mile) from the city centre. Count Giuseppe Panza, last owner of this frescoed 18th-century mansion, donated it to the nation in 1996. The interior is enhanced by an outstanding collecting of abstract American art, dating from the 1950s and strong on work from the 1980s and 1990s.

Classical versus contemporary

Rather than disperse his eclectic collection among his five sons, Panza left it to the Fondo per l'Ambiente Italiano (FAI), the Italian equivalent of the National Trust. As both a listed monument and

Varese, 'City of Gardens'

Farmer's market in Varese

an art gallery, the villa appeals to both lovers of contemporary art and fans of classical architecture. The former will appreciate the abstract tonal canvases, rooms bathed in brash neon light, bizarre installations and ceilings exposed to the elements. Classicists will admire the old Tuscan chests, Empire-style dining room and magnificent ballroom hung with chandeliers and subdued abstracts.

Lake Varese

Shaped like a battered boot, Lago di Varese is a small lake lying west of Varese. It is a gentle, unremarkable lake framed by rolling hills. From Biandronno on the western shore, you can cross to a tiny wooded island, Isolino Virginia, which has a restaurant and the remains of prehistoric pile-dwellings.

SACRO MONTE DI VARESE

If the weather allows, consider making a short visit to the Sacro Monte di Varese (Holy Mount of Varese) and the Parco Regionale di Campo dei Fiori. From Villa Panza return to Viale Arguggiari and head north along the same road for about 6km (3.75 miles), following the signs to Sacro Monte and Campo dei Fiori. A winding road climbs through the heart of Varese's villa zone, where the hills are dotted with *belle époque* and Art Nouveau concoctions perched on grassy knolls.

The **Sacro Monte di Varese** ➋ is a major pil-

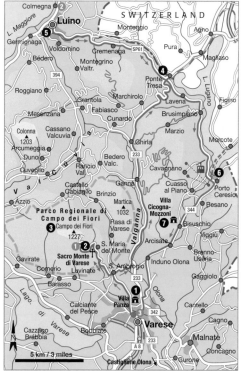

Lake Lugano

grimage site on the wooded slopes of Monte Campo dei Fiori. Along the steep Via Sacra are 14 devotional shrines with life-size terracotta figures and frescoes. From the **Santuario di Santa Maria del Monte**, and its village at the top, there are vertiginous views down over Lake Varese.

If you are in need of refreshment, stop for a drink and snack on the terrace of the **Al Borducan Ristorante Romantico**, see ❶, near the **Sacro Monte**.

Campo dei Fiori Regional Park

Continue another 5km (3 miles) beyond Santa Maria del Monte to the **Parco Regionale di Campo dei Fiori** ❸ (www. parcocampodeifiori.it) with six nature reserves and 16 marked trails. Almost at the top of the Campo dei Fiori mountain (1,226m/4,022ft) sits the G.V. Schiaparelli astronomical observatory, conceived by Salvatore Furia, who defused and detonated thousands of unexploded mines to build the road to the reserve.

LAKE LUGANO

From the park retrace your route, pass the Sacro Monte and take the first road on the left to join the SS233 to **Ponte Tresa** ❹ on Lake Lugano (27km/16.75 miles). The lake, which zigzags across the Swiss border, is wilder and less majestic than Lake Maggiore. Just over a third of the shoreline belongs to Italy, the rest to the Italian-speaking Swiss canton of Ticino. Steep wooded mountains rising sheer from the water pre-

clude development along most of the shoreline. Lugano is the only large town.

Ponte Tresa is a steamer stop and border village, packed at rush hour with Italian commuters travelling to and from Lugano. More peaceful and picturesque is the village of **Lavena**, set on a headland a couple of kilometres (1.25 miles) to the southeast.

Lunch in Luino

From Ponte Tresa, head west on the SP61 to **Luino** ❺ on Lake Maggiore. You could stop here for a lakeside stroll and lunch, or take the lakeshore road 2km (1.25 miles) north to Colmegna for lunch at the **Camin Hotel Colmegna**, see ❷. Encircled by woods, Luino was once a centre for smugglers, whose contraband coffee and cigarettes would pass between Switzerland and Italy as market forces dictated.

Porto Ceresio

After lunch head back to Ponte Tresa and follow the shore of Lake Lugano as far as **Porto Ceresio** ❻ (10km/6.25 miles), one of the most scenic drives in the province of Varese. A pretty Italian outpost, Porto Ceresio centres on an elegant harbour framed by steep shores. The name Porto Ceresio comes from the Latin name for Lake Lugano – Ceresio – which is still used by Italians.

If time permits, consider a ferry crossing from the Italian port to its Swiss rival across the water. The picturesque village of **Morcote** is set on the tip of the peninsula that runs down the

Campo dei Fiori in autumn

Sophisticated Porto Ceresio

lake towards Italy. Known as the 'pearl of Lake Lugano', it has a maze of alleys and is dominated by a medieval church.

VILLA CICOGNA-MOZZONI

From Porto Ceresio, take the SS344 south to Varese, stopping after 5km (3 miles) at Bisuschio to visit **Villa Cicogna-Mozzoni** ❼ (tel: 0332-471 134; www.villacicognamozzoni.it; Apr–Oct Sun and holidays 9.30am–noon, 2.30pm–7pm, other days by appointment; charge), an impressive Renaissance stately home inhabited by the genial Count Cicogna-Mozzoni.

The family fortunes were founded on a happy accident: in 1476 Galeazzo Sforza, the powerful duke of Milan, was out hunting when he chanced upon a bear on the rampage. He was saved from certain death by Agostino Mozzoni and his dog. To express his gratitude, the duke of Milan funded a scheme to transform Mozzoni's simple hunting lodge into this lovely villa, complete with Italianate gardens, formal box hedges and fountains.

Dinner options
If you are heading back to Varese, opt for the restaurant of the **Hotel Bologna**, see ❸.

see ❸.

Food and Drink

❶ AL BORDUCAN RISTORANTE ROMANTICO
Hotel Borducan, Via Beata Caterina Moriggi 43; tel: 0332-220 567; www.ristoranteborducan.com; Wed–Mon 8.30am–11pm, winter opening hours may be restricted; €
In an atmospheric Art Nouveau hotel this restaurant is famous for the Elixir Al Borducan that is also used to enhance historic recipes. Food is prepared according to the Bregonzio family tradition. Cuisine is inspired by seasonal ingredients, scents, and spices. From their terrace you can enjoy the view of the lakes as well as the massif of Campo dei Fiori, and a private garden.

❷ CAMIN HOTEL COLMEGNA
Via A. Palazzi 1, Colmegna (2km/1.25 miles north of Luino); tel: 0332-510 855; www.caminhotel.com; Mar–Nov Mon–Sat; €€
The hotel's two terraces overlook Lake Maggiore, which provides the ingredients for dishes such as carp in sweet and sour sauce and perch with tagliatelle. The villa was built in the early 18th century as part of a hunting estate and retains a large park with trails and a waterfall.

❸ HOTEL BOLOGNA
Via Broggi 7, Varese; tel: 0332-232 100; www.albergobologna.it; Sun–Fri; €
This popular hotel restaurant, in Varese's historic centre, offers hearty helpings of hams and salamis, fresh pastas, steaks, fish and creamy desserts. Booking essential.

Canova's 'Cupid and Psyche'

VILLA CARLOTTA AND BELLAGIO

Spend the morning exploring Villa Carlotta's gardens at Tremezzo, then catch a ferry to Bellagio, the 'pearl' of Lake Como, where you can wander the town's cobbled alleys and stroll in the grounds of Villa Serbelloni or Villa Melzi.

DISTANCE: Tremezzo to Bellagio by ferry: 3km/2 miles; walking in Bellagio: 2–4km (1.25–2.5 miles), depending on sites covered
TIME: A full day
START: Villa Carlotta
END: Bellagio
POINTS TO NOTE: If you are travelling to Villa Carlotta from Como (35km/22miles) allow 40 mins by hydrofoil or about 90 mins by ferry. The last hydrofoil back to Como from Bellagio leaves at around 8pm, earlier off-season. Bellagio is packed with restaurants but you could also consider a picnic in the gardens of Villa Carlotta (there are two allocated picnic areas).

CENTRAL LAKE COMO

The inspiration of writers, artists and composers, Lake Como is the most romantic of the three main Italian lakes. It has long been famed for its natural beauty, fine panoramas and sumptuous villas and gardens.

The lake is shaped like an inverted Y, caused by the division of an ancient glacier that carved out its valley. The three branches of the lake converge at the Punta Sparivento (the 'Point that divides the Wind'), the setting of famous Bellagio, 'pearl of the lake'.

Henry James was well aware of Lake Como's reputation for illicit trysts: 'It is commonly the spot to which inflamed young gentlemen invite the wives of other gentlemen to fly with them and ignore the restrictions of public opinion.' It was here, according to locals, that President Kennedy romanced Marilyn Monroe.

VILLA CARLOTTA

Villa Carlotta ❶ (www.villacarlotta. it; daily Mar–Sep 9am–7.30pm, late Sep–Oct 9.30am–6.30pm, late Oct– early Nov 10am–5pm; charge) has its own landing stage, but you can also access it via Tremezzo (450m/yds to the south) or Cadenabbia (1km/0.6 mile to the north), which has a car-ferry service.

Graceful Tremezzo   *Fresco detail, Villa Carlotta*

Graced by magnificent gardens, the villa was a wedding present from a Prussian princess to her daughter, Princess Carlotta of Nassau. Carlotta established a small court here, and completed the landscaping of the gardens in the 1860s. As a result, guests are greeted by a prosperous Baroque pile, bordered by a profusion of pink and white azaleas and a theatrical staircase that leads up to orange and lemon terraces.

Highlights

The villa inevitably plays second fiddle to the gardens; its large formal rooms contain a mixed collection of paintings and neoclassical statuary by Canova, including the *Cupid and Psyche*, symbol of the villa and a copy of the original in the Louvre.

Allow plenty of time for the gardens. There are 5.6ha (14 acres) and over 500 species of trees and shrubs, including 150 different varieties of azaleas and rhododendrons. The plants evoke an exotic map of the world: cedars of Lebanon, Egyptian papyrus, Japanese maples and banana trees, Chinese bamboo, Indian tea, Mediterranean agaves, ferns from New Zealand, eucalyptus and succulents from Australia and giant sequoias from South America.

Tremezzo

A short walk south is the resort of **Tremezzo**. While its heyday was in the 1930s, it retains a courtly grace, epitomised by the Grand Hotel Tremezzo. This delightfully mothballed affair remains popular for both wicked weekends and whirlwind gardening-club tours.

BELLAGIO

From Tremezzo frequent steamers cross the lake to **Bellagio ❷**. Walks around this cape afford sublime views of mountains in all directions, most notably north to the often snow-capped mountains along the Swiss border.

Keen walkers and hikers should pick up the pack of 18 itineraries in the province of Como, each with detailed information and map, from the tourist office on the lakeside. Other outdoor activities include motorboat-hire, rock-climbing and watersports.

On Bellagio's bustling waterfront, houses

Lakeside dining on Como

lead to a promenade lined with oleanders and limes. There are red-roofed
houses, pastel-tinged façades, steep
cobbled alleys, quaint craft shops, a
Romanesque belltower and lakeside
vistas.

Shopping along Salita Mella
To explore one of the prettiest alleys,
take the steep **Salita Mella**, just
opposite the passenger landing stage.
There are some enticing boutiques
here such as Ferrario at No. 10, selling hand-painted Como silk scarves
(the artist works in the shop) and gorgeous handbags. At Pierangelo Mas-
ciadri's shop, Arte e Moda, at No. 19,
you can buy beautiful scarves and
ties with designs inspired by classical mythology, Renaissance paintings
and rationalist architecture. Bill Clin-
ton, George W. Bush and Bill Gates
are among those who have commis-
sioned ties from Pierangelo – he has
thank-you letters to prove it.

Just before Pierangelo's shop, on
the left at No. 18, is **La Barchetta**,
see ❶, a good choice for regional cuisine if it is time for lunch.

Climb to the top of the street for Via
G. Garibaldi, the main shopping street
with leather and silk to suit all budgets and some very tempting delis.
The road leads to Piazza della Chiesa
with the much-restored Romanesque
Church of San Giacomo and a tower
that is all that is left of Bellagio's
medieval defence system.

Villa Serbelloni
For the best views from Bellagio, join an
afternoon tour of the gardens of **Villa
Serbelloni** ❸ (guided tours only with a
minimum of six people and weather permitting. Tours start from the medieval
tower in Piazza della Chiesa (mid-Mar–
mid-Nov Tue–Sun 11am and 3.30pm;
charge; for information: 031-951555,
info@promobellagio.it). Not to be con-
fused with the exclusive hotel of the same
name on the lake, the villa itself belongs
to the Rockefeller Foundation and is not
open to the public. The steep and winding path takes you high above Bellagio,
through fine gardens, for stunning panoramas of both sides of the promontory.

Villa Melzi
Having explored some of the steep alleys,
return to the lake. You can't get lost – all
the alleys lead down to the waterfront.
Turn left at the lake for a gentle lakeside
promenade, passing Bellagio's renovated lido, to **Villa Melzi** ❹ (Lungolario
Manzoni; www.giardinidivillamelzi.it;
end Mar–Oct daily 9.30am–6.30pm;
charge), an austere neoclassical villa set
in the first 'English' gardens on the lake.

Although the villa is a private residence and closed to the public, the
romantic grounds enchant visitors.
Beyond the entrance Japanese water
gardens are cleverly concealed from
the lake and an intimate mood is created by an ornamental pool, framed by
cedars, maples, camphor and myrrh.
On the grassy banks beyond rhododen-

The pastel-hued façades of Bellagio

drons and camellias create a blaze of colour in spring. Below, standing guard by the lake, is a quaint gazebo that captivated Stendhal and Liszt. Beside this bold folly, an avenue of plane trees leads along the shore to the small history museum in the orangerie, the villa, family chapel and Loppia landing stage.

Eating options

For lunch or dinner, avoid the waterfront tourist traps in favour of the best fish restaurant, **Silvio**, see ➋, a short walk from Villa Melzi, or **Bilacus**, see ➌, up from the waterfront. If you fancy an extravagant dinner on a luxury hotel's lakeside terrace, before a water-taxi ride home to reality, consider **Mistral** in the Grand Hotel Villa Serbelloni (see page 115). Otherwise, wait for a ferry in Bar Sanremo on the waterfront.

San Giovanni

In the hamlet of San Giovanni, the Museum of Navigation Instruments (Piazza Don Miotti; www.bellagiomuseo.com; 10am–1pm, afternoons by appointment only; charge) displays over 200 marine-themed exhibits, including antique sundials, compasses and 18th-century Venetian telescopes. The museum is about half an hour on foot in the Villa Melzi direction; alternatively, take the tourist train that departs from the ferry station and does a circuit of the peninsula.

Food and Drink

➊ LA BARCHETTA

Salita Mella 15; tel: 031-951 389; www.ristorantebarchetta.com; closed Tue, Oct–Apr; €€

Long-established lake-fish and seafood restaurant, situated up one of the steep, narrow alleys from the waterfront. You won't get the lakeside views, but there is a heated bamboo-covered terrace, service is friendly and the food (creative pastas, creamy risottos and delicious fresh fish) is a cut above the average eatery on the lake.

➋ SILVIO

Via Carcano 10–12, Bellagio; tel: 031-950 322; www.bellagiosilvio.com; €

This inviting modern fish restaurant above the gardens of Villa Melzi has wonderful lake views. It serves some of the freshest lake fish in Bellagio, caught by the family who run the restaurant. Reasonably priced rooms are also available.

➌ BILACUS

Salita Serbelloni 32; tel: 031-950 480; www.billacusbellagio.it; lunch and dinner Tue–Sun; €€

No lake views here but there is a delightful arbour for alfresco meals. This family-run restaurant offers attentive, friendly service and traditional no-frills cuisine.

Piazza Cavour, Como Town

COMO TOWN AND BRUNATE CABLE-CAR

Explore the historic quarter of Como on foot. Visit the glorious Gothic–Renaissance cathedral, hit the shops for fashion and silk, and take a cable–car ride to the village of Brunate for wonderful views across Lake Como.

DISTANCE: 6km (3.5 miles)
TIME: A half day
START/END: Piazza Cavour, Como Town
POINTS TO NOTE: If money is no object, make an advance reservation for dinner in the Villa d'Este (see page 116). Alternatively, a far cheaper option, which also requires advanced booking, is a night cruise from Como, with onboard dinner, dancing and live music. Night cruises depart from Como at 9/10pm in summer only (mid-June–Sept), normally on a Saturday. For details, see www. navigazionelaghi.it or call 800-551801 (free; within Italy only).

COMO TOWN

The biggest resort on the lake, **Como Town** is a somewhat disconcerting combination of a historic city and a bustling commercial centre. The town has a fine lakeshore setting, an interesting medieval quarter with cobbled, traffic-free streets and some lustrous shops, but there is nothing approaching the intimacy and timelessness of the small villages beside Lake Como. Whether or not Como conforms to your idea of the perfect holiday resort, it is a handy springboard for exploring the lakes region and has a magnificent setting at the end of the western arm of Lake Como.

Como Town's history

Since its earliest days, when it rose to prominence as a Roman town, Como has been an industrious, aspirational place. Como's most famous sons were Pliny the Elder (AD23–79), the Roman scholar who wrote the 37-volume *Historia Naturalis* (Natural History) and died during the eruption of Vesuvius in AD79, and his nephew and adopted son, Pliny the Younger (AD61–113), an author and lawyer, who is said to have owned at least two villas at Bellagio: one on the hilltop for study and reflection, and another on the lakeshore for hunting and fishing.

In the 11th century it became a free *comune* (city state), but in 1127 it was destroyed by Milan for having sided with Barbarossa, the German Holy Emperor. From 1335 Como came under the sway of the Milanese ruling dynasties, becoming famous for its silk production.

Como's cathedral

On the waterfront

The Romanesque style, which is particularly pronounced in Como, has been woven into the city's architectural fabric, from churches to fortified medieval towers. Many monuments also owe much to the craftsmanship of the *maestri comacini*, the medieval master-builders and sculptors of Como, who perfected the Lombard style and became renowned throughout Europe for their remarkable skills.

A TOWN WALK

Begin this walk around town at **Piazza Cavour ❶**, the city's waterfront square.

Como's Duomo

A little way inland along Via Caio Plinio II, **Piazza del Duomo** represents the best introduction to the medieval quarter, centred as it is on the splendidly solemn cathedral. The construction of the

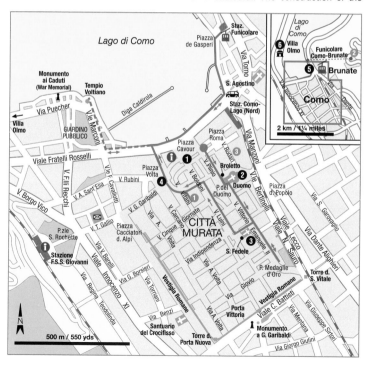

The basilica of San Fidele

Duomo ❷ (weekends 10.30am–5pm, holidays 1–4.30pm; Sat in July 9pm–11pm) began in 1396. Note the impressive gabled façade and observe how it spans the transition in style from late Gothic to Renaissance, with a richly sculpted main portal. Statues of Pliny the Elder and Pliny the Younger occupy the niches to the left and right respectively.

The interior is slightly gloomy but full of Renaissance works of art, including paintings by Gaudenzio Ferrari (c.1471/81–1546) and Bernardino Luini (1480–1532), two Lombard painters who were both influenced by Leonardo da Vinci.

Adjacent to the cathedral is the **Torre del Comune** (belltower), and the pink-, white- and grey-striped Gothic **Broletto**, the former town hall.

Piazza San Fedele

Take **Via Vittorio Emanuele II**, the main shopping thoroughfare, to Piazza Medaglie d'Oro, then head back towards the waterfront. If you want to take a break for a coffee at this point, check out Aida, a historic café and *pasticceria*, at No. 34 on the attractive medieval **Piazza San Fedele** (on the left as you head back along Via Vittorio Emanuele II). Overlooking the square stands the basilica of **San Fedele** ❸ (daily 8am–noon, 3.30–7pm), which was thought to be Como's first cathedral. The Lombard-Romanesque church was the work of Mestri Comacini, the medieval stonemasons of Como. It has been much altered over the centuries and was given a new façade in the early 20th century. Note the striking apse at the rear of the church.

Refreshment

From the square, continue towards the lake along **Via Luini**, crossing Via Cinque Giornate for **Bolla** at Via Boldoni 6, one of the best ice cream parlours in Como. Take the first left, and left again for **Via Vitani**. At No. 16, the **Osteria del Gallo**, see ❶, is ideal for a light lunch.

Piazza Volta

From Via Vitani turn left (east) into Via Muralto and follow the street to **Piazza Volta** ❹. Flanked by boisterous outdoor cafés, the square also has a statue of Count Alessandro Volta (1745–1827), a self-taught physicist who invented the battery and after whom the volt is named. In summer the square is a venue for concerts, as well as occasional sightings of George Clooney, Como's favourite adopted son.

If you wish to investigate Volta's legacy further, then walk to the western side of the harbour where you will find the neoclassical **Tempio Voltiano** (Volta Temple; Tue–Sun, Apr–Sept 10am–6pm, last admission 5.30pm, closed on Mon; charge). On display are Volta's personal effects and the batteries that he invented.

Sant'Abbondio

In a less salubrious area of Como, southeast of the centre, is the Romanesque

View over Como from Brunate

gem of Sant'Abbondio (Via Sant'Abbondio; daily 8am–6pm, winter 4.30pm). The apse is decorated with a remarkable cycle of mid-14th-century frescoes of the life of Christ.

BRUNATE

Return to Piazza Cavour. If the weather is fine, you might wish to take lunch in the environs of **Brunate**, which is set high above the city. Facing the water, turn right and follow the lakeshore north to **Piazza de Gasperi**, passing the city's most upmarket cafés and hotels. The **cable-car ⑤** to Brunate leaves every 15 to 30 minutes until midnight in summer, and the journey to the summit takes seven minutes. You can also walk up, along the Salita Carescione.

Once at the top, you can enjoy your lunch at the **Bellavista Hotel & Restaurant**, see ②, 150m/yds from the cable-car station. From Brunate there are outstanding views of the Alps, the lake and an array of 19th-century villas.

Evening stroll and dinner
In the evening join the throngs on a stroll along the waterfront from Piazza Cavour to the **Villa Olmo ⑥**, which is set in splendid Italianate gardens (winter 7am–7pm, summer 7am–11pm). Major art exhibitions are hosted at the villa from mid-March to the third week of July.

For dining, choose between the splendour of the **Villa d'Este** in Cernobbio, two ferry stops away, or Como's congenial **Sociale**, see ③, just north of the Duomo.

Food and Drink

① OSTERIA DEL GALLO
Via Vitani 16, Como; tel: 031 272 591; kitchen hours Mon 12.30–3pm, Tue–Sat 12.30–3pm/7–9pm; www.osteriadelgallo-como.it; €€
Simple, cosy, bistro-like trattoria with cockerel (*gallo*) ceramics and prints. Pop in for delicious wafer-thin slices of bresaola, plus home-made soups, pasta and cakes, and good cheeses and prosciutto.

② BELLAVISTA HOTEL & RESTAURANT
Piazza Bonacossa 2, Brunate ; tel: 031 221 031; www.bellavistabrunate.com; 12–3pm, 7–9.30pm, opening hours may vary off season; €€
The family-run Restaurant Bellavista offers regional dishes based on recipes from the local area. In the menu you will find a selection of dishes made with local products, meat specialities and fish from the lake. Reservations recommended.

③ SOCIALE
Via Rodari 6, Como; tel: 031 264 042; www.ristorantesociale.it; €€
Close to the Duomo, the popular Sociale occupies the Palazzo Odescalchi, which is embellished upstairs by frescoes of Constantine and a splendid Baroque fireplace. Classic local dishes.

Villa d'Este in Cernobbio

RAMO DI COMO AND VILLA DEL BALBIANELLO

Begin this tour with a romantic cruise along the beautiful Ramo di Como, past waterfront villas and gardens. After lunch on a haunted island, take a short boat trip to Villa del Balbianello, which has the finest setting on the lake.

DISTANCE: 60km (37-mile), ferry trip (return)
TIME: A full day
START/END: Como Town
POINTS TO NOTE: Check ferry times from any landing stage on the lake or on www.navigazionelaghi.it. If you plan to have lunch at the Locanda dell'Isola Comacina, reserve a table in advance and take plenty of cash (it is an expensive restaurant, and credit cards are not accepted). Before setting off, study the complex openings and access for Villa del Balbianello. Both the Locanda and the Villa del Balbianello are closed off-season.

RAMO DI COMO

From Como, catch a ferry that stops at Isola Comacina (the faster *aliscafo*, or hydrofoil, bypasses the island). Boats depart from **Piazza Cavour ❶** on the Como waterfront, where you can buy tickets. The cruise leads to the central part of the lake, famed for its villas and gardens. En route it criss-crosses the most beautiful arm of Lake Como, the **Ramo di Como**, moving from the sunny western side to the shady eastern side. The west has the best resorts, historic villas and gardens; the wilder east is dotted with Roman-esque churches and the odd silk factory. This cruise starts at Como, but Isola Comacina and Lenno are also accessible from Bellagio, Tremezzo or any of the ferry stops on the Como–Colico service.

Celebrated villas

On the western shore, **Cernobbio ❷** is the first major resort after Como. The town has an appealing lakefront and old quarter, but the most eye-catching sights are the 19th-century **Villa Erba**, which belonged to the family of film director Luchino Visconti before becoming a conference centre, and the **Villa d'Este**, the most prestigious hotel in the lakes (see page 66).

After **Torno ❸**, on the eastern side, you can glimpse in the distance the som-

Yachts and jetties   *Laglio*

bre **Villa Pliniana**, where Byron, Stendhal and Liszt stayed, and where Rossini composed the opera *Tancredi* (1813).

Romantic **Moltrasio** ❹, back on the sunny side of the lake, features the deceptively low-key **Villa Le Fontanelle**, designed as a perfect setting for fashion shows. This was the favourite home of the late Gianni Versace (he had four altogether) – and the one where he chose to be buried. The villa was reg-ularly visited by a string of celebrities. After Versace's death it was sold to a Russian multimillionaire.

Laglio

The Hollywood star George Clooney bought the Villa Oleandra in the tranquil village of **Laglio** ❺ in 2002. (The chances are there will be someone on your boat pointing out the beautiful 25-room mansion on the waterfront.) Clooney fell in love with the villa on a motorcycling holiday around the Alps. House prices in the vicinity have been soaring ever since. To thank Clooney for putting Laglio on the map, its mayor has made the actor an honorary citizen of Laglio.

AMALFI COAST

The 'Amalfi Coast', so named because its dramatic cliffs and wild atmosphere are reminiscent of the real Amalfi Coast near Naples, begins just to the north of Torno, on the eastern shore.

The fine Romanesque church in **Pognana Lario** sits in the shade of surrounding villas,

Isola Comacina, the only island on Lake Como

while **Nesso**, also on the shaded side, is known for a long Roman-esque bridge and a gloomy five-storey silk factory that closed in the 1950s, when silk production moved to China, Brazil and Turkey. From Nesso, the ferry crosses to **Argegno** ❻, with its red-tile roofs and sunny lakefront. Perch abound in this, the lake's deepest section.

ISOLA COMACINA

Tiny **Isola Comacina** ❼ is the only island in Lake Como. Alight here if you are planning to eat at the **Locanda dell'Isola Comacina**, see ❶. It gets very busy at weekends, so aim to be there at 1pm for lunch, or 8pm for dinner.

The island becomes a focus of attention during the **Festival of San Giovanni** (St John), the most magical festival in the lakes, celebrated on 24 June.

On the far shore of the lake is the blighted fishing village of **Lezzeno**, in contrast to splendid **Bellagio**, which commands the point beyond. Due to the gigantic shadow cast by the mountains, the sun is permanently blotted out, and the locals pay the price in terms of tourism.

Haunted island

Tiny though it is, Isola Comacina became a political and military centre in the Middle Ages, acquiring the name of Crispoli, City of Gold. But the island was cursed by the bishop of Como in 1169, probably in revenge for its alliance with Milan, and Como's

---

Villa d'Este

The Villa d'Este was built in 1568, when Cernobbio was a village of fishermen and woodcutters. In 1815 Caroline of Brunswick – princess of Wales and future queen of England – fell in love with Lake Como, and persuaded the owner, Countess Pino, to sell her the villa. Caroline spent five years at the Villa d'Este, following a disastrous marriage to the Prince of Wales (the future King George IV). The couple had found each other equally unattractive (he had married 'the vilest wretch this world was ever cursed with' to pay off his debts), and within a year they were living apart. Caroline spent her time embellishing the villa, and leading a lavish and, by all accounts, lascivious lifestyle.

Having run up debts, she returned to London in 1820 in an abortive attempt to take her place on the throne. Legally, Caroline remained Queen Consort until she died at the age of 53. Unlike George IV, she had been popular with the London public, as she had been with the locals of Cernobbio.

Since 1873 the Villa d'Este has been the most luxurious hotel on the lake, hosting royalty, politicans and film stars, and maintaining the elegance of a bygone era. The restaurant offers a less-expensive way to live it up for a while.

Comacina church

soldiers razed its churches and forced the inhabitants to take refuge in Varenna. The Baroque **Oratorio di San Giovanni** and the ruins of medieval churches are all that remain. More recently, the island was bequeathed to Belgium's King Albert I, who donated it to the state in 1927. Today it is under the supervision of Milan's Brera Academy of Fine Arts.

Exorcising the demons

In 1949 a passing English journalist by the name of Frances Dale apparently came up with the idea of a 'rite of fire' exorcism to stimulate the tourist trade – and the word spread like wildfire. Today guests at the Locanda are welcomed by the current melancholy master of ceremonies, the bobble-hatted Benvenuto Puricelli (who was born in Sala Comacina, facing the island, and who served a stint as head chef at London's Penthouse Club). Puricelli has been exorcising the island's demons on a daily basis for the past 30 or so years, in which time the roster of visiting international celebrities has included Sylvester Stallone, Michael Schumacher, Madonna, Arnold Schwarzenegger, Brad Pitt and Elton John. The inn's gallery is full of portraits of such stars participating in the theatrical 'purification ceremony'.

Set meal and ceremony

For all the hokum, the set meal – ranging from an array of *antipasti* to chunks of Parmesan, baked onions, grilled trout, chicken and orange ice cream – is good. The rite of fire begins at the flambéed-coffee stage, and involves arcane incantations and copious amounts of brandy and sugar. Even if the ceremony is not your cup of capuchin, the lakeside views are simply gorgeous. After lunch you may want to follow a path that passes the ruins of the Romanesque churches sacked in 1169.

Good alternative options for lunch off the island are the **Locanda La Tirlindana**, see ❷, by the landing stage where boats cross to Isola Comacina, or **Trattoria Santo Stefano**, see ❸, on the main square in Lenno.

VILLA DEL BALBIANELLO

Set on the tip of a wooded promontory between Lenno and Sala Comacina, **Villa del Balbianello** ❽ (www.fondoambiente.it; mid-Mar–mid Jan Tue, Thu–Sun 10am–6pm, last entrance to villa 4.30pm; compulsory guided tours, charge) enjoys the loveliest setting on the Italian Lakes. Romance, peace, seclusion, tranquillity and fabulous gardens: this ochre-coloured villa has everything you might hope to find in the region.

To access the villa, you can get a boatman at Isola Comacina to ferry you across, or take the public ferry to nearby Lenno, where you can be taken across in the private shuttle

Villa del Balbianello

boat (look for the sign at the landing stage). Another option, if it is a Tuesday, Saturday, Sunday or public holiday, is to walk from Lenno to the villa (about 1km/0.6 mile; signposted from the church square).

A cardinal's retreat

In 1786 the sybaritic Cardinal Durini bought the villa here as a retreat from his taxing diplomatic missions. He incorporated what remained of a medieval Franciscan convent, which, with its quaint pair of belltowers, you can still see today. After landscaping this rocky spur, he enlarged the villa, and, as his crowning achievement, added the loggia on the highest point. Durini wanted both a memorable venue for literary salons and a place from which to admire the sun setting in the mountains.

> ### The A list
>
> Lake Como is a haven for celebrities, who tend to be discreet and whose privacy is respected. George Clooney has a lovely waterfront villa at Laglio; Sting and Ryanair owner Michael O'Leary have homes on the lake. Guests of the late Gianni Versace at his villa in Moltrasio included Madonna, Elton John and Bruce Springsteen, but, like many of the most desirable lakeside residences these days, the villa was sold to a Russian multimillionaire.

The most recent owner of the villa was the wealthy explorer Count Guido Monzino, a descendant of the cardinal. Acquiring the property in 1954, the count restored the villa and filled it with his collection of books, furniture and works of art. On his death in 1988, he left the villa, complete with contents, to the FAI (the Italian National Trust). Famous for his mountaineering feats and Arctic expeditions – he led a North Pole expedition in 1971 and the first successful Italian ascent of Everest in 1973 – he turned the villa into an international centre for the study of explorations.

Visits of the **villa** take in the library, with hundreds of books devoted to explorations, and a museum full of mountaineering memorabilia, including the sledge on which Monzino trudged to the North Pole in 1971. Fine though the interior is, more impressive is the **loggia** when seen from outside: it is covered in climbing plants, and an old fig tree clings to its columns.

The villa has featured in numerous films set in the region. For more on this, see page 137.

Romantic gardens

The **garden** makes the most of its setting on a rocky spur and the poor soil conditions. Somewhere between a classical 18th-century Italian affair and a romantic English garden, it exploits the gnarled outline of the barren rock to present beguiling paths

Romantic balcony

The sumptuous view from the villa

that lead up to a three-arched folly. Bound by boxwood and laurel hedges, pergolas, climbing plants and scented wisteria, this secret garden is mirrored in the lake. Cypresses, holm-oaks and plane trees pruned into candelabra shapes provide shelter for snowdrops, cyclamen and magnolia. Closer to the villa are lakeside vistas framed by terracotta tubs of pink hydrangeas and classical statues that protrude from beds of azaleas.

The final view is of the Italian flag unfurled on the jetty, in keeping with Monzino's will. The explorer wanted the gesture to be 'in memory of all the flags my Alpine guides placed on countless peaks all over the world'.

Unless you are up for more adventures, you should ask the boatman to drop you off at the Lenno jetty, where you can take a ferry home.

Food and Drink

① LOCANDA DELL'ISOLA COMACINA

Isola Comacina; tel: 0344-55083/56755; www.comacina.it; closed Nov–Feb and Tue off-season; €€€

Even if the food was not a draw, people would still flock here to the Locanda for its exclusivity and the bizarre 'rite of fire'. The set menu of regional food has hardly changed since the restaurant opened in 1947. You can reach here via the public ferry or the island boat service from Sala Comacina. No credit cards.

② LOCANDA LA TIRLINDANA

Piazza Matteotti, Sala Comacina; tel: 0344-56637; http://www.latirlindana.it; summer daily, winter Thu–Tue; €€

Facing Isola Comacina, this charming little *locanda* draws food-lovers from afar. Frederic extends a warm welcome, while Patricia produces mouth-watering *ravioli al limone*, *lavarello con pancetta dorata* (flatfish from the lake in breadcrumbs and bacon), succulent fillet of beef with gorgonzola sauce, and *marquise al cioccolato* to die for. On a warm day arrive early to secure a seat on the terrace, which has glorious views across to the island.

③ TRATTORIA SANTO STEFANO

Piazza XI Febbraio 3, Lenno; tel: 0344-55434; Tue–Sun, may be closed Jan–Feb; www.santostefanolenno.it; €€

A small sought-after trattoria where chef Giovanni Sansone produces delicious lake fish-based dishes at affordable prices. Menus change according to the availability of the freshest ingredients, but are likely to feature chub pâté, smoked trout, ravioli stuffed with mixed lake fish, grilled whole fish, or *missultitt* – small fish that are dried and salted, then fried with vinegar, oil and parsley, and served with slices of polenta.

The Bartolomeo Colleoni coat of arms

BERGAMO

Bergamo has it all: a majestic setting, a magnificent medieval town, designer shops and gourmet restaurants. This tour takes in one of Italy's richest art museums, then explores the historic Upper Town's piazzas and monuments.

DISTANCE: 4.5km (2.75 miles)
TIME: A full day
START: Accademia Carrera
END: Il Sentierone
POINTS TO NOTE: Avoid driving and parking within Bergamo. There are direct train services from Milan or Como, or, if you are killing time before a flight, buses run every 20 mins from the nearby Orio al Serio airport (10–15 mins). They stop at the railway station, city centre and funicular station for the Upper Town. Bergamo has a tourist office at Piazzale Guglielmo Marconi, in the Lower Town and another in the Upper Town at Via Gombito 13. There is also an office at the airport (Mon–Sat 8am–8pm, Sun 10am–6pm). The ATB System (www.atb.bergamo.it) is a transportation system for travelling within the city of Bergamo and the 29 surrounding towns by bus, funicular train and the T1 Bergamo-Albino tramway.

Seen from afar, Bergamo is a mass of belltowers and domes silhouetted against the Alps. Originally settled by Celts and Romans, the town nevertheless has a Venetian soul, following 400 years of Venetian rule. There are two centres: the historic *Città Alta* (Upper Town) and the more modern *Città Bassa* (Lower Town). The former is bound by a circle of 16th-century walls built by the Venetians after the city expanded beyond its medieval ramparts and fortress.

LOWER TOWN

This walk begins in the Lower Town, laid out in the 1920s with stately tree-lined avenues, porticoes and piazzas.

Accademia Carrara and GAMeC

The **Accademia Carrara** ❶ (Piazza G. Carrara 82; www.lacarrara.it; Wed–Mon 9.30am–5.30pm, closed on Tuesdays; Special opening days: 25 April, 1 May; charge) has a fine collection of Lombard and Venetian art, amassed by a local aristocrat in the 18th century. Among the treasures in this neoclassical palace are Gothic works by Pisanello, and Renaissance and Mannerist works by Bellini,

Busy Via Colleoni   *View down to the Lower Town*

Veronese, Tiepolo, Tintoretto, Raphael and Mantegna.

Opposite the Carrara is the **GAMeC** ❷ (Galleria d'Arte Moderna e Contemporanea; Via San Tomaso 53; gamec.it; Wed–Mon 10am–6pm, closed on Tue; charge for main exhibitions), hosting temporary art exhibitions.

UPPER TOWN

From the Carrara, follow Via della Noca east through the Venetian gateway **Porta Sant'Agostino**, take the Via Porta Dipinta in front of the ex-convent of Sant'Agostino, and climb up into the heart of the **Città Alta**. **Via Gombito** ❸, a lively medieval street lined with food shops and eateries, leads into Piazza Vecchia, near to the home of Bgigi on Via Gombito, see ❶.

Piazza Vecchia

A showpiece of both medieval and Renaissance monuments surrounding a fountain with marble lions, the **Piazza Vecchia** ❹ is often described as the most perfect square in Italy.

Flanking the square is the **Palazzo della Ragione** (Feb 1–Oct 31 Tue–Sun 9am–7pm, Nov–Jan 31 Tue–Sun 9am–6pm, closed on Mondays; charge), the much-remodelled medieval council chambers, decorated with a winged Lion of St Mark, the symbol of the Venetian republic. An elegant external stairway leads up to the **main hall**, which houses a collection of fresco panels taken from deconsecrated churches

and convents in the region. The Palazzo is displaying some of its major works.

The glass lift of the **Campanone** (Belltower; Nov–Mar: Tue–Fri 9.30am–1pm, 2.30pm–6pm, Sat and holidays 9.30am–6pm; Apr–Oct: Tue–Fri 10am–6pm, 10am–8pm; closed on Mondays charge) whisks you up to the top of the tower for fine views. The belltower chimes 180 times daily at 10pm, in memory of the curfew under the Venetians.

Near the square is Da Franco Ristorante with excellent pizza (see page 116).

Basilica of Santa Maria Maggiore

The religious heart of the town is the adjacent **Piazza del Duomo** ❺, home to both the hybrid **Duomo** with an 1886 façade, and, submerged beneath a sumptuous Baroque interior, the Romanesque basilica of **Santa Maria Maggiore** (Mon–Wed 9am–12.30pm, 2.30–6pm, Thu–Sun and holidays 9am–6pm). The church has a beautiful Gothic porch adorned with statues and reliefs, and an interior profuse with gilt, stuccowork and paintings.

Donizetti

Bergamo-born composer Gaetano Donizetti (1797–1848) is commemorated in the city by a street, theatre, memorial, monument and museum: the Museo Donizettiano (Via Arena 9; Tue–Fri 10am–1pm, Sat and holidays 10am–1pm/3–6pm) south of the Cittadella.

Donizetti's piano

Colleoni Chapel

Adjoining the church is the ornate **Cappella Colleoni** (Mar–Oct daily 9am–12.30pm, 2–6.30pm, Nov–Feb Tue–Sun 9am–12.30pm, 2–4.30pm), built in 1472–6 as a mausoleum for Bartolomeo Colleoni, a rich Venetian *condottiere* (mercenary), who demolished the sacristy of Santa Maria Maggiore to create the space.

A masterpiece of the early Lombard Renaissance, this mausoleum has a marble façade embellished by medallions, columns, sculpture and reliefs. The interior shelters ceiling frescoes by Tiepolo and the tomb of the *condottiere*, surmounted by a gold equestrian statue. The tomb on the left is that of his daughter, who died at the age of 15.

Inspect the railings of the Colleoni Chapel and you will see Colleoni's coat of arms. Called '*i tre colleoni*', the gleaming crest comprises three testicles (*coglioni*)

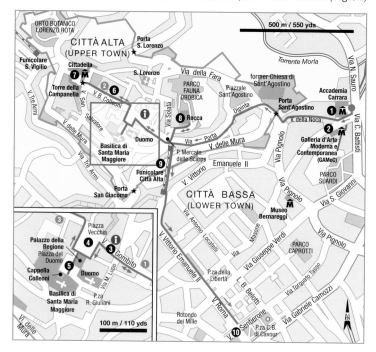

The Duomo's Baroque ceiling   *Colleoni Chapel*

– the third endowed by mother nature.

Museums of Archaeology and Natural History

Return to Piazza Vecchia and head west along **Via B. Colleoni** ❻, the continuation of Via Gombito. **Da Mimmo**, see ❷, and **Vineria Cozzi**, see ❸, are good pitstops for lunch or dinner.

At Piazza Mascheroni, pass under the Torre della Campanella for the **Cittadella** ❼. This was built in the 14th century as a fortress to defend the west section of the city, then converted by the Venetians as a residence for captains and sailors. Today it is home to the rather dry **Museo Archeologico** (Apr–Sep 9am–12.30pm/2.30–6pm, Sat and holidays 10am–1pm/2.30–6pm, closed on Mon) and **Museo di Scienze Naturali** (Oct–Mar 9am–1pm/2–5pm, Sat–Sun and holidays 10am–6pm; closed on Mon).

La Rocca

Retrace your steps back past the cathedral and along Via Gombito to Piazza Mercato delle Scarpe. If you have time, divert left from the piazza along Via alla Rocca and climb up to the 14th-century **Rocca** ❽, built on the foundations of the Roman Capitol by the Visconti and reinforced by the Venetians. This is the highest point of the city, with fine views.

Via Solata, home to Officina Dei Sapori (see page 116), is worth a visit.

FUNICULAR TO LOWER TOWN

To return to the lower town, take the 120-year old **funicular** ❾ from Piazza Mercato delle Scarpe. The funicular drops to Viale Vittorio Emanuele II. From here walk southeast to the tree-lined Il **Sentierone** ❿, a favourite rendezvous for the locals and a popular spot for an evening stroll.

Food and Drink

❶ BGIGI

Via Gombito 26; tel: 346 181 6145; Mon–Fri 7.30am–7.30pm, Sat–Sun 9am–11pm; €
This place offers breakfasts, lunches, snacks and drinks. Vegetarian friendly with vegan and gluten free options.

❷ DA MIMMO

Via Colleoni 17; tel: 035-218 535; ristorantemimmo.com; Wed–Mon lunch and dinner, Tue dinner; €€

Two of the seven Mimmi sons carry on the family tradition, producing honest Bergamasque cuisine, including excellent home-made pasta. The setting is a 14th-century palace and a garden that can accommodate 200 diners.

❸ VINERIA COZZI

Via Colleoni 22a; tel: 035-238 836; www.vineriacozzi.it; open daily for lunch and dinner; €
An inviting wine bar with a huge choice of Italian wines and a menu of *antipasti*, pasta, vegetarian dishes, cold meats and cheeses.

LAKE ISEO

Explore the town of Iseo before cruising to the lovely island of Monte Isola for a lakeside stroll and lunch. An afternoon tour of the lake takes in the wild western shore and lakeside villages that retain their medieval core.

DISTANCE: Driving tour: 72km (45 miles)
TIME: A full day
START/END: Iseo
POINTS TO NOTE: Check timetables and cruise details at the Iseo tourist office on the waterfront (Lungolago Marconi 2; tel: 030-3748733). The tour of the lake by car is just as lovely by ferry.

Unfairly neglected in favour of the larger lakes, **Lake Iseo** (Lago d'Iseo) is more tranquil and less self-consciously quaint. The lake is short on the beautiful attractions that are a hallmark of the other lakes, but compensates with a gentler way of life, fine walks and a delightful unspoilt island to explore.

ISEO

The best base from which to explore the lake is **Iseo ❶**, an attractive historic town that has not completely sold out to tourism. Until the 1870s it was a signif-

icant port that shipped grain from Valle Camonica and steel from the industrial lakeside ports. Today it is a commercial town on a smaller scale. Sandwiched between the waterfront and the feudal Castello Oldofredi, it retains its cosy medieval street pattern and an elegant lakeside promenade.

Historic centre

The liveliest part of town is the porticoed **Piazza Garibaldi**, dominated by a statue of the great patriot perched on a mossy rock – this is one of the few horseless statues of the Risorgimento leader. In Piazza Mazzini, reached by a narrow alley, you can see old stone washtubs and the Arsenale that today serves as an art exhibition venue. Take Via Sombrico and Via delle Pieve for the church of **Sant'Andrea**. Although clumsily remodelled, it has the finest Romanesque belltower in the region. To the southwest, the restored 15th-century **Castello Oldofredi** is set on a mound and is home to the little **Museo delle due Guerre** (Museum of the Two Wars; Sat–Sun 9am–noon,

Lake Iseo at dusk

3–6pm), where two rooms house equipment used in World Wars I and II, including military uniforms, firearms and hand grenades.

MONTE ISOLA

Return to Piazza Garibaldi and make for the lakeside, where you can take a relaxing ferry ride to **Peschiera Maraglio ❷** on **Monte Isola**, usually the second stop. The mountainous, densely forested island – the largest lake island in Europe – supports a 200-strong community of fishermen, boatbuilders and net-makers.

Car-free island

The pace of life is palpably slow here: private cars are banned (though local motorbikes are not) and a minibus service connects the various hamlets. The fishing hamlets reveal refined touches, from sculpted portals to tiny courtyards and loggias. Above, tiers of olive groves merge into vineyards and chestnut groves. The highest peak is surmounted by the 16th-century **Santuario Madonna della Ceriola**, built over a pagan shrine.

Lunch at Peschiera Maraglio

Choose a typical lakeside haunt at Peschiera Maraglio (which is also known simply as 'Peschiera') for an outdoor lunch. After you have had your fill of grilled sardines, perch risotto and lake scampi, check out the cluttered shop on the waterfront that sells fishing nets and hammocks: net-making is an integral part of life on the island. An industry thought to have been initiated by Cluniac monks 1,000 years ago

View over Marone

now embraces Wimbledon tennis nets and World Cup football nets. Depending on the season and time of day, there may be signs of boatbuilders at work or fishermen laying their catch out to dry in the sun.

Peschiera to Sensole

The best gentle walk from Peschiera west is along the lakeside path to **Sensole ❸**, taking in views of competent swimmers competing for attention with struggling ducks. Both hamlets are set on the sunny side of Monte Isola, and the view encompasses the tiny island of San Paolo with the town of Iseo melting into the background. If you have not already eaten, you might consider **La Spiaggetta**, see ❶, between the villages. The alternative to walking is to hire a bike at Peschiera – you can cycle round the whole island in about 50 minutes.

WESTERN SHORE

Catch the ferry back to Iseo, then take a scenic drive clockwise round the lake (following signs west to Sarnico) to see Riva di Solto's rugged western shore in Bergamo province.

Clusane

Just to the west of Iseo, **Clusane ❹** is a food-lover's paradise: on the waterfront there are fine fish restaurants that specialise in baked tench. Crowned by a castle, Clusane overlooks a busy port full of traditional red- and yellow-rimmed fishing boats setting out in search of tench, pike, chub and lake sardines. The village borders wine-growing Franciacorta, and its hinterland is dotted with inns. You may wish to return to Clusane for dinner.

Sarnico to Riva di Solto

The first resort on the western shore (5km/3 miles), **Sarnico** occupies the site of a prehistoric stilt village and owes much of its character to the ruined medieval ramparts and graceful loggias. But it is best known for its speedboat companies that support one of the lake's premier activities.

Follow the lakeshore road for 20.5km (12.75 miles) to Riva di Solto. From over-quarried Tavernola Bergamasca to Riva di Solto lies the most dramatic stretch of the western shore, with coves carved into limestone cliffs and sheer ravines running down to gnarled rocks. These jagged formations reputedly inspired Leonardo da Vinci's *Virgin of the Rocks* and possibly the *Mona Lisa*.

Riva di Solto ❺ is a pretty fishing hamlet full of alleys and arches, with placid views across to the domesticated shore of Monte Isola.

Lovere

After 7km (4.5 miles) is **Lovere ❻**, dominating the northern end of the lake. Originally a Venetian textile town, Lovere turned to steel then watersports tourism. Stroll along the

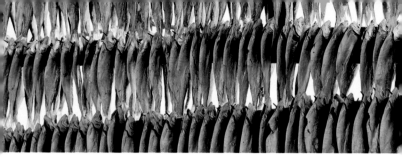

Lake fish hanging out to dry

waterfront with its lakeside cafés and restaurants, and then explore the historic core with its narrow alleys, medieval towers, castle remains and the frescoed Renaissance church of **Santa Maria in Valvendra**.

On the lakefront, the neoclassical Palazzo Tadini is home to the Galleria dell'Accademia Tadini (Via Tadini 40; www.accademiatadini.it; May–Sept Tue–Sat 3–7pm, Sun 10am–noon, 3–7pm, Apr and Oct Sat 3–7pm, Sun 10am–noon, 3–7pm; charge), displaying works of the Lombard and Venetian schools, including Tintoretto, Jacopo Bellini and Giandomenico Tiepolo.

EASTERN SHORE

The eastern shore is less peaceful, and between Pisogne and Marone you will be driving through tunnels. Pisogne can be clearly seen across the water from Lovere, but has to be accessed by taking the main Via Nazionale (SS42) north, beyond the northern tip of the lake, and then heading south along the SP55, signposted to Pisogne.

Pisogne

The former arms-manufacturing town of **Pisogne ❼** was a centre of commerce for the whole valley in medieval times, and retains an appealing historic centre. The main square is the spacious **Piazza del Mercato**, overlooking the lake and flanked by arcades. Looking onto the square is

The Camonica Valley

North of Lake Iseo, the Camonica Valley (Valle Camonica, www.turismovalleca-monica.it) has been inhabited since the Neolithic era. As long ago as 8,000BC hunters were recording scenes of every-day life by carving on the smooth sand-stone rocks of the valley floor. Some 180,000 etchings have been discov-ered, constituting the greatest concen-tration of prehistoric rock carvings in Europe. These are scattered all along the valley, but the best examples are contained within Capo di Ponte's Parco Nazionale delle Incisioni Rupestri (National Park of Rock Engravings; Tue–Sun 8.30am–1 hour before sunset, Oct–Feb until 4.30pm; charge), a Une-sco World Heritage Site.

Although the Camonica Valley is now-adays partially marred by industry, the park is rural and wild, with birch and pine woods. The primitive carvings span several thousand years, from Stone Age scratchings to Bronze Age narratives to Roman graffiti. Animals – from Etruscan boxer dogs masked as cockerels to elk speared by hunters and deer caught in lassoes – feature prominently. However, unless you are an expert or have booked a guide (tel: 0364-42140 at least two days in advance, around €80 for half a day), the mysteries can be hard to deci-pher, and the routes are not as clearly marked as you might expect from a World Heritage Site.

Fresco of 'The Last Supper' in the church of Santa Maria della Neve in Pisogne

the medieval **Torre del Vescovo** (Bishop's Tower), where (according to one of the rather finely illustrated information panels in the town centre) those who defaulted on taxes were hung in a cage fixed to the tower, and where, in 1518, eight women accused of witchcraft were imprisoned before being burned alive in the square.

Chiesa di Santa Maria della Neve

On the outskirts of the town (follow signs for 'Affreschi del Romanino'), the church of **Santa Maria della Neve** (Tue–Fri 2–6pm, Sat–Sun 10am–6pm, typically reduced hours in winter) is known as 'La Cappella Sistina dei Poveri' (the Poor Man's Sistine Chapel) on account of the striking frescoes covering the walls and ceiling. Depicting scenes from *The Passion of Christ*, the works are by Romanino (c.1484–1559), a leading Brescian Renaissance artist known for his realistic portraits – which can be found all around Lake Iseo.

Food and Drink

● LA SPIAGGETTA

Via Sensole 26, Monte Isola; tel: 030-988 6141; Wed–Mon, closed evenings; €
This little family-run trattoria serves simple fish dishes on the lakeside path between Sensole and Pescheria Maraglio. Lunch only; no credit cards; booking advisable.

Zone Nature Reserve

Continuing 10km (6.25 miles) south along the lake you come to **Marone**, overlooking the diminutive, privately owned **Isola di Loreto** (Loreto Island), where trees cluster around a castle.

A twisting road inland from here takes you to **Zone** (7km/4.25 miles), a picturesque village renowned for the **Riserva Naturale Piramidi di Zone** ❽. This unique formation of 'erosion pillars', created by uneven glacial erosion, is the finest example in Europe. Their most unusual features are the boulders that are precariously perched on top, looking like hats. The best views of these 'stone fairies' (as the locals call them) is at **Cislano**, before you get to Zone.

Dinner options

Return to Marone and follow the road south for Iseo (13km/8 miles) to complete the circuit.

For dinner, shoot past Sulzano, unless you intend to take the ferry back to Monte Isola for another fish feast (the ferry only takes 15 minutes from here). Clusane is a better bet than Iseo for dining out. A good option is **Punta dell'Est** (see page 116). Alternatively, walk or drive inland from Clusane 1.5km (1 mile) for the enchanting **Relais Mirabella** (see page 117), signposted from the main road.

Another lovely setting with first-class food is the **Relais I Due Roccoli** (see page 117), at Polaveno, 12km (7.5 miles) east of Iseo.

Franciacorta vineyard

THE FRANCIACORTA WINE TRAIL

This leisurely drive in the prestigious wine-growing region of Franciacorta takes you through rolling vine-clad hills, past castles, villas and wineries. The trip starts with a visit to a Cluniac monastery and ends with dinner in Clusane.

DISTANCE: 60km (37 miles)
TIME: A half day
START: Iseo
END: Clusane
POINTS TO NOTE: The majority of the wine estates require prior notice for visits and are only open on specific weekends. The Iseo tourist office (Lungolago Marconi 2; tel: 030-374 8733) has all the necessary information including maps of the Strada del Vino and can make reservations for you. Alternatively, contact the Associazione Strada del Vino Franciacorta, the local wine-growers' association (www.franciacorta.net), which can arrange visits to wineries for individuals or as part of a tour. Castello di Bornato medieval fortress and wine estate is open on Sundays and holidays mid Mar–Nov, but needs prior notice if you are visiting at other times. For La Montina you must always book in advance. There are also routes for cyclists and walkers, ranging from two to three hours to a couple of days.

The scenic Franciacorta region south of Iseo is renowned mainly for sparkling wines, but also dry, velvety whites and medium-bodied reds. The rolling countryside is dotted with manor houses and villas, many of which have been transformed into wine estates or inns.

Free Court

In the 11th century local nobles called on Cluniac monks to drain the land around Franciacorta. The results were beneficial to both parties: the local economy received a boost, and the way was paved, literally, for the building of impressive new monasteries. The ecclesiastical authorities appreciated the local climate and countryside to the extent that the village of Borgonato became the summer residence of monks from Brescia's Santa Giulia monastery. The secular authorities granted tax concessions, which led to the region's nickname of Corte Franca (Free Court). This in turn encouraged patrician families from Brescia and beyond to build villas in the mellow hills here. Wealthy restaurateurs and viniculturists followed in their wake, and Franciacorta was on

Monastery of San Pietro in Lamosa

the way to becoming the sought-after retreat it is today.

NATURE RESERVE

Coming out of Iseo take a right turn on to the old road to Brescia (avoiding the newer SP510). You will soon see the **Riserva Naturale Torbiere del Sebino ❶** on your right. This former peat bog is the watery domain of tench, trout and eel. It is also home to a variety of predatory birds, from herons to kingfishers. You can stroll along the paths that go through the peat bogs.

SAN PIETRO IN LAMOSA

Towards the southern end of the reserve is the little Cluniac monastery of **San Pietro in Lamosa ❷** (officially 3–6pm, but erratic). It sits on a small rise on the right above the road (it is roughly 5km/3

miles from Iseo and easy to miss, so go slowly). Comprising four chapels, the monastery was founded in the 11th century and added to over the centuries. Sadly it has been neglected, but volunteer restorers in recent years have revealed a number of frescoes – some dating back to Gothic times.

FRANCIACORTA WINE TRAIL

Monticelli Brusati

Head south to Camignone, then follow the marked Franciacorta wine route (marked Strada del Vino Franciacorta) east to **Monticelli Brusati ❸** and vineyards that stretch out as far as the eye can see. The village is home to **La Montina** winery (Via Baiana 17; tel: 030-653 278; lamontina. com; for the tour hours contact the office Mon–Fri 8.30am–12.30pm, 2–6pm) set around the beautiful Villa Baiana. Monticelli Brusati is also the splendid setting for the **Azienda Agricola Villa** wine estate (follow signs for Villa), complete with farm-stay homes and a restaurant (tel: 030-652 329; www.villafrancia-corta.it) that serves pasta, fresh *antipasti* and superb wines.

Many wine estates open for tours and tastings during the Festival of Franciacorta in mid-September.

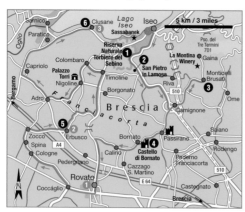

| Bornato Castle | Restored fresco in San Pietro |

Bornato

Retrace your route to Camignone, then drive southwest to **Passirano**, home to a striking medieval castle. Follow signs for the next village, **Bornato**, where the **Castello di Bornato** ❹ (Via Castello 24; www.castellodibornato.com; mid-Mar–mid-Nov Sun and holidays 10am–noon, 2.30–6pm; charge) has wonderful views of Franciacorta. A crenellated medieval castle, it opens onto a Renaissance villa and Italianate gardens. This is a small wine estate, with tasting included in the visit.

Erbusco

If lunch is now a consideration, you could stop at the **Trattoria del Gallo**, see ❶, at **Rovato**, or head on to **Erbusco** ❺, the unassuming stone-built village at the centre of the wine district. Here you can dine and drink as the locals do at **Cadebasi**, see ❷.

Corte Franca

After Erbusco, still following the wine route signs, you reach **Corte Franca**, the heart of the wine region, consisting of four villages: Borgonato, Timoline, Colombaro and Nigoline. Among the mansions in this region is Nigoline's 18th-century **Palazzo Torri** (tel: 030-982 6200; Sun only 3–6pm, by reservation only; charge), decorated with fine antiques and frescoes.

DINNER IN CLUSANE

A return to the lakeshore at **Sarnico** marks the end of the route. En route to Iseo, you could stop at the fishing village of **Clusane** ❻, known for its baked-tench cuisine. **Trattoria Al Porto**, see ❸, in the centre, just back from the lake, is recommended.

Food and Drink

❶ TRATTORIA DEL GALLO

Via Cantine 10, Rovato; tel: 030-724 0150; www.trattoriadelgallo.it; closed on Wed; €€

This retro-looking trattoria serves simple Brescian cuisine. Typical dishes are steak, rabbit or horse, pastas with *funghi* or truffles, or meat-filled ravioli in a buttery sage sauce. Reserve.

❷ CADEBASI

Via Cavour 11, Erbusco; tel: 030-836 7340; Fri–Sun lunch and dinner, Mon, Wed, Thu dinner, closed on Tue; €€

This new to town restaurant is popular with locals and travellers alike. Their extensive wine and drink menu pairs perfectly with bar snacks and mains.

❸ TRATTORIA AL PORTO

Porto dei Pescatori, Clusane; tel: 030-989 014, www.alportoclusane.it; closed on Wed; €

This inviting trattoria by Lake Iseo has been run by the same family since 1862. It is renowned for *tinca al forno* (baked tench) with polenta, as well as other freshwater fish.

Aerial view of Sirmione

SIRMIONE

Explore Sirmione, steeped in history and enticingly set on a finger–like peninsula pointing into the southern end of Lake Garda. This walk takes you from the fairytale Scaligeri castle to the evocative ruins of the Grottoes of Catullus, one of the finest Roman patrician residences in northern Italy.

DISTANCE: 3.5km (2 miles)
TIME: A half day
START/END: Rocca Scaligera
POINTS TO NOTE: Sirmione's Old Town is prohibited to traffic except for residents and hotel guests, so park as near as you can to the entrance by the drawbridge. In season and on Fridays (market day) and Sundays this could be in a car park 10–15 mins walk away. A little electric train links the centre with the Grotte di Catullo, though it's not far to walk. Be prepared for narrow alleys packed with tourists, especially from May to September. Pick up a map and other information from the tourist office (tel: 030-374 8721) near the entrance of the historic centre at Viale Marconi.

The Romans were drawn to the invigorating waters around Lake Garda and, impressed by Sirmione's hot, sulphurous springs, developed the spa as a sybaritic retreat. The conquering Scaligeri counts from Verona recognised Sirmione's military potential, and built a medieval fortress from which to govern the southern part of the lake. From the 15th until the end of the 18th century the town was subject to Venetian rule. In spite of recent over-commercialisation, it retains much of its architectural grace.

ROCCA SCALIGERA

To enter the historic quarter, cross the drawbridge over the duck and fish-filled moat for the 13th-century **Rocca Scaligera ❶** (Piazza Castello; Tue–Sat, 8.30am–7.30pm, Sun 8.30am–1.30pm, holidays 8.30am–7.30pm, closed on Mon; charge). Crowned by swallow-tailed battlements and encircled by water, the fort has guarded the entrance to the historic centre for eight centuries. It was built by the Veronese Scaligeri dynasty, who ruled Verona from 1260–1387. In addition to the moat, the castle features well-preserved bastions and crenellations, and a fortified dock. The main attraction is wandering around the battlements and climbing up the towers

Piazza Carducci

Crossing the drawbridge of the Rocca Scaligera

for views. A recognisable feature of the tyrannical Scaligeri dynasty are castles with fishtail battlements. Sirmione's Rocca Scaligera is a fine example, but there are several others dotted round Lake Garda.

Opposite the castle you will find the tiny 14- to 15th-century church of **Santa Anna della Rocca**. It was also constructed by the Scaligeri family,

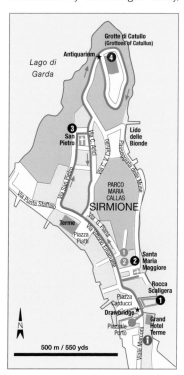

and for centuries served as a place of pilgrimage.

VIA VITTORIO EMANUELE

From the castle follow the flow along Via Vittorio Emanuele, the main street leading northwards, and take the first right by the Bar Scaligeri, then under the arch and right again for the pretty 15th-century church of **Santa Maria Maggiore ❷** (free), which overlooks a pebble beach. The church has a pretty portico which incorporates a Roman capital. The lakeside promenade by the beach provides a peaceful route to the Grottoes of Catullus for those who prefer to steer clear of the crowded centre. Follow the beach to the Lido delle Bionde (9am–11pm, may be closed off-season; charge), where you can swim in the lake, take out a pedalo or have a snack at the café. The Grottoes of Catullus are signposted from the lido. When the lake water is low you can walk right round the peninsula below the grottoes.)

On the same street as the church you will find **La Fiasca**, see ❶. The surrounding web of tiny alleys abounds in gelaterias, overpriced art galleries, souvenirs and outlets selling chic handcrafted jewellery.

Spa centre

Via Vittorio Emanuele continues northwards to the modern spa centre of **Terme di Sirmione** (www.termedisir-

Remains of the Grottoes of Catullus

mione.com; winter break: two weeks in January; charge) on Piazza Piatti. Here the hot sulphur springs – bubbling waters are channelled up from the bottom of the lake – are utilised in the

Sirmione's spas

In 1889 a Venetian diver called Procopio inserted a long pipe into the lake rocks near the Grottoes of Catullus, and released a jet of hot sulphurous water. The discovery led to the delicate operation of laying 300m (984ft) of pipes to bring up the steaming waters from the bottom of the lake. Sirmione's first spa centre opened in 1900, and today around 650,000 guests arrive annually for treatment. The waters are rich in sodium chloride, bromine and iodine, and are used for treating respiratory and rheumatic diseases, as well as for beauty and well-being programmes. The Terme combines spa centres and four hotels with thermal facilities. The Aquaria wellness centre offers access for two or five hours plus a variety of day pass programmes (up to 6 days), where you can make the most of thermal pools, bubbling beds, hydro-massage, and aromo-chromatic showers. Alternatively, if you want to spare the expense and time, just pop into a pharmacy and purchase a bottle of Acqua di Sirmione or Sirmiogel – both composed of 100 per cent Sirmione spa water.

treatment of an assortment of respiratory complaints.

Church of San Pietro

From Piazza Piatti take Via Punta Staffalo, which leads to the western shore. Turn right along Via San Pietro, a turning to the north, which brings you to the church of **San Pietro ❸**. This Romanesque church, the oldest in Sirmione, was constructed on top of the remains of a Roman temple, and remodelled with recycled Roman bricks.

A lane links the church to the Via Caio Valerio Catullo, leading north to the Grottoes of Catullus.

GROTTOES OF CATULLUS

Around the end of the promontory, medieval Sirmione can be explored to its Roman core. Crowning the rocky top of the peninsula, and once reached via a triumphal arch and barrel-vaulted arcades, the **Grotte di Catullo ❹** (Via Catullo; winter time Tue–Sat 8.30am–5pm, holidays 8.30am–2pm, summer time Tue–Sat 8.30am–7.30pm, holidays 9.30am–6.30pm; closed on Mon; charge) are the remains of a vast Roman villa and spa complex, constituting one of the most important examples of a Roman patrician residence in northern Italy.

The site was named after Rome's greatest lyric poet, who was said to have languished here when rejected by

The view from the ruins   *Unwind at Terme Catullo*

Lesbia, his mistress in Rome. However, although the pleasure-seeking poet makes reference to a home in Sirmione close to his heart, the general consensus of opinion is that this villa dates from a slightly later period.

The ruins

Marking the entrance to the ruins is a museum (winter time open 8.30am–7.30pm, rest of the year hours are as Grottoes of Catullus), which displays some beautiful fresco fragments and mosaics discovered at the villa, along with grave finds and sculptural fragments from other parts of Sirmione.

The ruins cover some 2ha (5 acres) of the promontory and are set high above the lake amid olive and cypress trees. A geometric puzzle, the ruins reveal a complex interplay of passages and porticoes – a sensitive blending of brick and rough-hewn stone. The most imposing remains are on the north side, with rooms up to 12m (39ft) long. Deciphering the rooms on the various levels is not easy, but there are plaques on the site showing how the villa was constructed, what the rooms were for and how it would have looked in all its glory. In any event, it is lovely just to wander round the ruins and admire the views.

EATING OPTIONS

For restaurants, head back towards the castle. If your feet are weary at the end of the day, take the little **Trenino Elettrico** (electric train), which provides a shuttle service (for a small charge) between the Grottoes of Catullus and the Terme Catullo at Piazza Piatti.

Sirmione is packed with take-away pizza places but for proper food in a pretty setting try **Al Torcol**, see ❷ or splash out on gourmet fare at **La Rucola** (see page 119), close to the castle. If you are taking a ferry home, you might be tempted to wait for your boat at the **Risorgimento** (see page 119), on Piazza Carducci where the ferries depart.

Food and Drink

❶ LA FIASCA

Via Santa Maria Maggiore 11; tel: 030-990 6111; lunch and dinner Thu–Tue, may be closed off-season; www.trattorialafiasca. it; €

This central trattoria is a cut above the average tourist Sirmione fare. No-frills classics, regional dishes and home-made pastas are served.

❷ OSTERIA AL TORCOL

Via San Salvatore 30; tel: 030-990 4605; €€

Authentic home-cooked fare at reasonable prices make this a rare find for tourist-packed Sirmione. It is small, family-run and highly popular. Book in advance if you can, ideally for the vine-clad garden on a warm evening.

Touring the lake by boat

LAKE GARDA CRUISE

Lake Garda's scenery is enormously diverse, from the sea-like southern basin, fringed by beaches, to the fjord-like north, where the Brenta Dolomites drop sheer into the water. This full-day cruise takes in Riviera-like shores, lakeside villages and historic castles and harbours.

DISTANCE: Hydrofoil from Sirmione to Malcesine: 60km (37 miles); return trip: 120km (75 miles)
TIME: A full day
START/END: Sirmione
POINTS TO NOTE: Make an early start and take one of the fast routes (marked in red on the timetable – available from the tourist office at the entrance of town) to get to Malcesine for lunch. The boat will make several stops en route, but you will only have time to disembark at one destination other than Malcesine. Recommended are either Gargnano or Bardolino. If you are limited to half a day, concentrate on the lower lake only. This trip starts at Sirmione, but you can also go from other resorts on the southern shore, such as Desenzano del Garda or Peschiera del Garda.

Approximately 51km (32 miles) long and 17km (10.5. miles) wide at its maximum point, Garda is Italy's largest lake. Apart from some spectacular scenery, it offers fine beaches and clean, warm waters. The area enjoys a wide range of climatic conditions, from chilly Alpine glaciers north of the lake to Mediterranean warmth.

In the Middle Ages ruling dynasties built splendid defences around the lake's shores; in the 19th century European aristocrats and literati came for the healthy climate. Although picturesque villages still dot the shorelines and medieval castles rise from the waters, it is nowadays the most crowded of the Italian lakes, with large numbers of German and Austrian holidaymakers, sailors and windsurfers descending on its shores. The south in particular has seen major commercialisation.

Cruising the lake is far more relaxing than coping with traffic-filled lakeshore roads and dimly lit tunnels. It is also the best way to admire the scenery.

BARDOLINO

From the ferry landing stage off Piazza Carducci in **Sirmione** ❶, take the fast

Shaft of sunlight over the waters of Garda

service to **Bardolino** ❷ on the Veneto shore, framed by rolling hills and vine-clad slopes. Ideally, wait until the return trip for a visit here, when you can enjoy the eponymous wine in any of the local bars. Bardolino Superiore now has DOCG status; to learn more about the delicious cherryish-red wine, visit the excellent **Museo del Vino** (Wine Museum; Via Costabella 9, Bardolino; www.museodelvino.it; Apr–Oct daily 9am–12.30pm, 2.30–7pm, Nov–Mar daily 8.30am–12.30pm, 2.30–6.30pm). In the adjoining Zeno winery you can taste whites and rosés as well as the reds, and purchase bottles from two or three euros.

Bardolino is also home to the **Museo dell'Olio di Oliva** (Olive Oil Museum; Via Peschiera 54, Cisano di Bardolino; Mon–Sat 9am–12.30pm, 2.30–7pm, Sun 9am–12.30pm), with a shop selling olives, honey and pasta, as well as olive oil. Wine and food aside, the town has a ruined castle, two Romanesque churches and a medieval quarter.

GARDA

The lake took its name from the town of **Garda** ❸, which shelters in the lee of a huge rocky outcrop. Lake Garda was once called Benacus (Beneficient) – and it is occasionally still referred to by the Latin name. The former fishing village is now a popular resort, with a long café-lined promenade that you can see from the boat, and narrow alleys packed with *trattorie* and souvenirs.

Gargnano, a sailing centre

THE LIMONI RIVIERA

From Garda the boat crosses the lake to **Gardone Riviera** ❹ and **Salò** ❺, two prestigious resorts on the Lombardy bank, whose elegant promenades you can admire from the boat. (If you have time another day, they are covered in detail in route 16; see page 90).

Lemon terraces

The boat now skirts the loveliest stretch of coast, where wild Alpine terrain stretches all the way to **Riva del Garda**. Despite the cliffs, the area is a hothouse for Mediterranean shrubs

---

Limone sul Garda

Several boats, including a car ferry and private excursion boats, link Malcesine with the busy resort of Limone on the Lombardy shore. Less self-consciously cute than Sirmione, Limone is caught between lush Mediterranean vegetation and sheer rock faces that cower under snow-clad peaks. D.H. Lawrence adored Limone, which, he wrote, overlooked 'a lake as beautiful as the beginning of creation'. What was once an old fishing port is today a tad touristy. You might assume the village is named after the citrus fruit, but it is more likely that the name derives from the Latin *limen* (border), referring to the former frontier here between Austria and Italy.

---

and citrus fruits as a result of the balmy microclimate.

Citrus fruits, introduced by medieval monks, used to constitute the lake's cash crop. To protect the lemons from rare but catastrophic cold spells, the terraces were traditionally south-facing, covered with wooden supports in the colder months, and watched over by gardeners who would light fires if the temperature dropped suddenly. Citrus cultivation went into an irreversible decline in the 19th century, with competition from cheaper citrus fruits grown in the hotter climate of southern Italy. These distinctive but mostly defunct *limonaie* (lemon terraces), with their rows of white stone pillars, still dot the lakeshore from Gargnano, north of Gardone, to **Limone sul Garda**. The Limonaia del Castel in Limone (Apr–Oct daily 10am–6pm, end of May–mid Sep 10am–10pm, winter time Fri–Sat 10am–5pm; nominal charge) and the Limonaia Prà dela Fam in Tignale (Apr–Oct for opening hours contact 0365 73354; nominal charge) are two of the few that have been preserved and can be seen in operation.

Gargnano

From Gardone it is a short hop to **Maderno**, twinned with neighbouring **Toscolano**, and used mainly by tourists for its car ferry service across to **Torri del Benaco** on the opposite side of the lake. Going north, **Gargnano** ❻ is one of the main sailing centres on

Drinks at Limone sul Garda   *Rock faces beside the town*

the lake. Remarkably unspoilt, it has a lively little port, a promenade of orange trees, some charming hotels and several gourmet restaurants. With time in hand, alight here and take a leisurely stroll before boarding the next boat to Malcesine.

MALCESINE

Alight at family-friendly **Malcesine** ❼, the loveliest resort on the Veneto shore, with a café-lined waterfront, balconied Venetian-style houses and a maze of cobbled alleys. Choose from one of the many restaurants, ranging from simple *osterie*, such as **Santo Cielo**, see ❶, to gourmet haunts such as **Trattoria Vecchia Malcesine**, see ❷, and **Ristorante Re Lear** (see page 119).

Scaligero Castle
The village clusters below the crenellated **Castello Scaligero** (daily Mar–Nov 9.30am–6.30pm; 045 6570333; charge), whose battlements and tower command fine views of the lake. Within the walls is a **natural history museum**.

Monte Baldo Cable-Car
Behind the resort you will find Malcesine's modern **funicular** (www.funiviedelbaldo.it; every 30 mins Mar–mid-Nov 8am–6.45pm, mid–Oct–mid–Nov reduced hours; charge), which links the resort to the summit of **Monte Baldo** (2,218m/7,275ft). The panoramic rotating cable-cars whisk you up there in a matter of minutes, stopping en route at San Michele. The mountain ridge offers spectacular views, scenic walking trails and a profusion of flora. In winter the cable-car goes up to the ski slopes.

Cruise back to Sirmione, alighting, if you haven't already, at Bardolino en route.

In late September and early October Bardolino hosts the Festa dell'Uva (Grape Festival) where corks pop nonstop.

Villa in Gardone Riviera

GARDONE RIVIERA

On the western shore of Lake Garda, Gardone Riviera maintains much of the elegance that drew the rich, royal and famous in the late 19th century. A visit to botanical gardens and Il Vittoriale degli Italiani, the most eccentric residence on the lakes, is followed by a ferry trip to the historic resort of Salò.

DISTANCE: Gardone Riviera to Salò by ferry: 4km (2.5 miles)
TIME: A half day
START: Gardone Riviera
END: Salò
POINTS TO NOTE: If you are not driving, there are regular ferries to Gardone Riviera from Sirmione, Desenzano del Garda or Peschiera del Garda. Villa Fiordaliso restaurant requires advance reservations for lunch or dinner. If a trip to Isola del Garda appeals, check out the times of boats from Salò and book a guided tour in advance. If the tour is in the morning, start at Salò and visit Gardone Riviera in the afternoon.

It was the mild climate that attracted the Austrian emperor and other members of the European elite to build palatial villas here in the 1880s, as **Gardone Riviera** became the most fashionable resort on the lake. It retains luxury hotels, some fine villas, a promenade lined with oleanders, palms and orange trees, and a beach for lake swimming. The guest list at the *belle époque* **Grand Hotel** ❶, which stands prominently on the waterfront, includes Somerset Maugham, Vladimir Nabokov and Winston Churchill.

GIARDINO ANDRÉ HELLER

Just off the lakeside promenade, the **Giardino André Heller** ❷ (www.heller garden.com; Mar–Oct daily 9am–7pm; charge) is an oasis of flora created in 1912 by Arturo Hruska, a passionate botanist and dentist to the last czar of Russia. It is a peaceful spot with pretty rockeries, English and Japanese gardens, and an Alpine garden with ravines chiselled out of the rocks.

IL VITTORIALE

Take a left turn after the botanical gardens and climb up to **Gardone Sopra**, the oldest part of town. This is the site of a much-visited, somewhat bizarre villa, secluded by cypresses and oleanders. **Il Vittoriale degli Italiani** ❸ (www. vittoriale.it; winter time Vittoriale Park

Hruska Botanical Garden   *Mausoleum of Gabriele d'Annunzio*

9am–5pm, Sat–Sun until 5.30pm, guided tours of house 9am–4pm, museums 9am–4.45pm, Sat–Sun until 5.15pm, summer time Vittoriale Park 9am–8pm, guided tours 9.30am–7pm, museums 9am–7.30pm; house closed Mon, war museum closed Wed; charge) is a testament to the megalomania of Gabriele D'Annunzio (1863–1938). A soldier, poet, Fascist, aviator, aesthete and womaniser, he occupies an odd place in Italian hearts, somewhere between reverence and bafflement. 'Destiny calls me towards Lake Garda,' he declared, although it was actually Mussolini who presented him with the villa in 1925.

The dictator and the poet
Disillusioned with the paltry gains won by Italy in the post-World War I peace – the Dalmatian town of Fiume (Rijeka; now part of Croatia) on the Adriatic had been promised to Italy but was presented to Yugoslavia instead – D'Annunzio and his private army occupied Fiume. Forced to withdraw in 1921, D'Annunzio retired to Lake Garda.

Decadent decor
Named in celebration of Italy's victory over Austria in 1918, and remodelled by D'Annunzio, the 18th-century Il Vittoriale is one of Italy's most flamboyant pre-war estates. The house, known as the **Prioria**, has two reception rooms, one cold and formal for disliked guests (including Mussolini),

the other a warmer chamber where his favourites were welcomed. D'Annunzio's delusions of grandeur led him to create a low entrance to his study so guests had to stoop, presumably to bow. D'Annunzio abhorred daylight, so the windows were made of stained glass or painted over. When the penumbra became too much to bear, D'Annunzio would retreat to the coffin in the Sala di Lebbroso.

The **Museo della Guerra** (War Museum) documents D'Annunzio's military enterprises, displaying uniforms, medals for bravery, banners and numerous photographs.

Isola del Garda

Off the headland south of Salò is the Isola del Garda (Garda Island). For centuries this was a monastery island, and the first religious community was said to have been founded on the island by St Francis of Assisi. Since the dissolution of the monastery by Napoleon, the island has been in private hands. The present owners are the Cavazza family. When Count Cavazza died he left the island to Lady Charlotte Chetwynd Talbot and her seven children. It is open to two-hour-long guided tours (tel: 328 612 6943 for advance bookings – essential; Mar–Oct; www.isoladelgarda.com; charge). Boats leave from several harbours in the lower lake, including Salò.

Yachts at Salò

Relics of the Fiume Fiasco

The splendour of the grounds contrasts with the ugliness of the creations that inhabit them: a magnolia grove houses a war memorial, while the *Puglia* ship that featured in the Fiume fiasco is bizarrely beached among the cypresses. In a hangar are a biplane that flew over Vienna in the war, vehicles that took part in the Fiume debacle, and the Italian flag. The mausoleum, where Fiume casualties are buried, features D'Annunzio's kitsch, self-aggrandising tomb, and, displayed in an eerie museum, his death mask.

Lunch options

For lunch the **Agli Angeli**, see ❶, is a good family-run restaurant, handy for Il Vittoriale; or, if cash is no consideration, head for the **Villa Fiordaliso** (see page 120). After lunch, drive or take the ferry to Salò (10 minutes on the fast service, 13 mins on the normal ferry).

SALÒ

Set on a beautiful deep bay with a long lakeside promenade, **Salò** is an appealing combination of bustling local town and elegant resort. It was founded in Roman times, then in 1337 became the capital of the Magnifica Patria, a community of 42 towns. During a less fortunate episode of its history, Salò was the seat of Mussolini's puppet republic in 1943 – his last desperate attempt to reorganise Fascism in Italy. A town of fleeting moods rather than awesome sights, it wears its history lightly. After an earthquake in 1901 the resort was rebuilt in airy Art Nouveau style, and is still graced by elegant villa-hotel restaurants. One of the loveliest is the Villa Isabella, now the Hotel Laurin (Viale Landi 9; hotellaurinsalo.it). This was the headquarters of the Italian Foreign Ministry, presided over by Mussolini.

Stroll along the **Lungolago Zanardelli** ❹ (the lakeside promenade). The

Emmental at the market   *Shopping street*

waterfront near the centre has some fine arcaded buildings, including the **Palazzo della Magnifica Patria**, the 17th-century town hall.

The most prominent landmark of Salò is the lofty campanile of the late Gothic **Duomo ❺** (daily 9am–noon, 3.30–7pm; free) on the waterfront towards the eastern end of the Lungolago Zanardelli. The church has an elaborate Gothic altarpiece and a number of Renaissance paintings.

For lunch or dinner in Salò, try the **Osteria dell'Orologio**, see ❷, or **Osteria di Mezzo**, see ❸.

Food and Drink

❶ AGLI ANGELI

Via Dosso 7, Gardone Riviera; tel: 0365 20991; www.agliangeli.biz; Wed–Mon; €€
A cosy old-world *locanda* near Il Vittoriale, with a terrace for summer dining. Typical dishes are leek flan, risotto, pasta with local Bagoss cheese, duck with pepper and grapes, and lake fish. Although the menu changes month to month.

❷ OSTERIA DELL'OROLOGIO

Via Butturini 26, Salò; tel: 0365-290 158; typically closed two weeks in Jan and July; €€
The emphasis here is on traditional dishes such as bean soup, *osso buco*, hearty stews and fish sourced from the lake.

❸ OSTERIA DI MEZZO

Via di Mezzo 10, Salò; tel: 0365-290 966; www.osteriadimezzo.it; noon–9.30pm; closed on Tue; €€
One of Salò's best restaurants, set in vaulted cellars in the centre. Serves salamis, homemade pasta, *baccala* (dried cod), perch, pike or eel from the lake, rabbit, beef and delicious cheeses.

Riva del Garda

A TASTE OF TRENTINO

Riva del Garda is Trentino's gateway to Lake Garda, and the castles of Arco, Drena, Toblino and Tenno are all a short drive away. Riva's picturesque location and healthy climate drew the European aristocracy from the early 1800s. Today it is a popular tourist resort.

DISTANCE: 60km (37 miles)
TIME: A leisurely day
START/END: Riva del Garda
POINTS TO NOTE: If lunching at Castel Toblino (Toblino Castle), be sure to make a reservation. In summer occasional evening cruises depart from Riva; for information visit www. navigazionelaghi.it or tel: 800-551 801 (free; within Italy only).

RIVA DEL GARDA

If arriving in Riva by car, park near the castle, ideally in the car park by the waterfront, the Giardini di Porta Orientale, or the adjoining Congress Centre.

As a medieval port for powerful prince-bishops, **Riva del Garda ❶** became a pawn in the dynastic struggles between such city states as Milan, Venice and Verona. In 1703, during the War of the Spanish Succession, the port was sacked by the French, leaving Riva a shadow of its former self. Like the rest of Trentino, Riva was revived under Aus-

trian rule (1815–1918), and it flourished as a fashionable resort, attracting such Mitteleuropean literary heavyweights as Franz Kafka, Thomas Mann and Friedrich Nietzsche. Contemporary Riva draws large numbers of tourists: middle-aged ones off-season, and, in summer, a younger crowd who enjoy the watersports as much as the culture.

Wine country

Thanks to its microclimate, Garda Trentino is favourable to wine-growing, and vineyards are abundant. The most noteworthy grape is the Nosiola, which produces dry white wines and Vino Santo Trentino. The latter is a sweet dessert wine made with grapes that are dried out on wooden racks and then pressed during Holy Week, before being aged for three years in oak casks.

Rocca di Riva

Begin your tour of Riva at the lakeside **Rocca**, the moated medieval castle upon which the resort is centred. This austere military stronghold, which once included an arsenal, barracks and palace, evokes

only a partial sense of its former glory. The Rocca was designed as a fortress, but the Renaissance prince-bishops of Trento turned the interior into a patrician residence. It was further domesticated during Austro-Hungarian times, when its fearsome appearance was compromised by the lowering of its corner towers.

Beyond the drawbridge, the **Riva del Garda Museo** (Piazza Cesare Battisti; Mar–Nov 10am–6pm, closed Mon; Jun–Sep daily 10am–6pm; charge) has a minor art collection, sculpture from regional churches and archaeological finds going back to the Bronze Age.

Piazza Cavour

After the Rocca you might hit a lakeside café, or, from the adjoining Piazza Garibaldi, take Via Mazzini to **Piazza Cavour**, the main inland square, which is often obscured by market stalls. Here, you can buy local olives, cheese and wine at the Wednesday market; to sample Riva's best coffee, head for Bar Pasticceria Maroni.

Piazza 3 Novembre

Return to the Rocca and head west to the main **Piazza 3 Novembre**, which opens onto the lake. The square is lined with 15th-century Venetian-Lombard palaces, including the town hall. With its 13th-century gateway, a view of the 16th-century bastion above, and **Hotel Sole**, once an Austro-Hungarian rulers' residence, the square is a microcosm of Riva's history. The hotel has lost much of its grandeur, but its sunny terrace is good for drinks and people-watching.

For spectacular views over the lake, take the lift up the **Torre Apponale** (Dec, Jan, Feb closed; Mar–Nov 10am–6pm, closed Mon; charge). The tower has variously served as a prison, as a store for salt and grain, and as a look-out point during World War I.

TORBOLE

When you are ready to leave Riva, set off east along the main SS240 for 4km (2.5 miles) to **Torbole ❷**. Presenting the less genteel face of Lake

Arco Castle

Garda, what was once a fishing village is now a lively watersports centre that benefits from unusual wind conditions. Just before midday, the Ora southern wind whips down the lake and fills the sails of windsurfers until early afternoon.

If lunch is a now priority, you could try the Trentino specialities at Torbole's **Piccolo Mondo**, see ❶, by the River Sarca, or, if you fancy lunch in Castel Toblino, start driving north following signs for Arco and Trento.

Alternatively, the footpath from Riva to Torbole (4km/2.5 miles) along the waterfront affords fine lake and mountain views. Goethe described Torbole as 'a wonder of nature, an enchanting sight'. The setting is as alluring as ever, but the village is rather spoilt by the main coastal road slicing through. However, this is no deterrent to hikers, free climbers, paragliders, windsurfers or sailing enthusiasts who descend on Torbole all year round.

ARCO

After 5km (3 miles) you come to **Arco** ❸, a spa once favoured by Austro-Hungarian grand-dukes, and renowned for its gardens and pleasant climate. In the late 1800s the resort was characterised by *belle époque* balls, health cures and carriage rides.

The former archducal gardens overlook the wizened stump of the **Castello di Arco** (Apr–Sep 10am–7pm,

Mar and Oct 10am–5pm, Nov–Feb 10am–4pm, from Jan 7th open only Sat–Sun 10am–4pm; charge), which looms above the resort. A steep path winds up to the castle, but the interior, for all its fragments of Gothic frescoes depicting courtly scenes, does little justice to the striking setting.

DRENA AND TOBLINO CASTLES

Continuing 18km (11 miles) north to Toblino, you will see on the right (beyond Dro) **Castello di Drena** (Mar–Sept Tue–Sun 10am–6pm, July–Aug Tue–Sun 10am–7pm, Oct Tue–Sun 10am–5pm, Nov–Dec 10am–5pm, Feb Sat–Sun only 10am–6pm, closed Jan; charge). The stark late-12th-century castle, controlling the Sarca and Cavedine valleys, was destroyed in 1703, but has undergone restoration in recent years. Today it serves as a venue for exhibitions and conferences. A museum contains local archaeological finds.

Castel Toblino ❹ (www.castelto blino.com), set on the tiny lake of the same name, and with an atmospheric restaurant, seems to materialise from nowhere. Diners at the **Ristorante Castel Toblino** (see page 119) can visit the atmospheric interior, complete with Renaissance courtyard and 17th-century stoves. Others can enjoy a glass of wine in the bar/café below (8.30am–9pm), with a lovely terrace overlooking the lake.

Cycle race through the streets of Arco

Adamello-Brenta Park

Retrace your path to Sarche and take the first right turn – towards Comano Terme. The start of this western route skirts the **Parco Adamello-Brenta**, named after the Brenta rock formations, a Dolomite group marked by towering limestone pinnacles and surfaces bathed in a pink-tinged orange sheen. Toblino's vineyards give way to neat barns and lush Alpine pastures, deep forests and sheer rock faces.

THE ROAD TO RIVA

Comano Terme ❺ is a thriving spa resort, with its curative waters gushing out of the rocks at 28°C (82°F). Next head for **Bleggio Superiore** ❻ (5.5km/3.5 miles), a rambling village in a lovely Alpine setting, well signed from Comano Terme.

From Bleggio follow the signs for **Fiavè** ❼ (5km/3 miles), which has an **archaeological site** mired in the bogs just outside the village on the Riva road and the Museo delle Palafitte di Flavè, dedicated to prehistoric pile dwellings. The nature reserve features the remains of a late Neolithic village.

Continue on the Riva road (the SS421) to **Lago di Tenno** ❽ (11.5km/7 miles), a lake formed by a landslide. The medieval village of **Tenno** ❾ clustered around a private castle, lies 3km (2 miles) to the south.

From here the road twists down to Riva del Garda. On the approach to Riva, the reappearance of olive groves represents the clearest shift back to the sultry Mediterranean microclimate of Lake Garda.

Dinner in Riva

For dining options in Riva del Garda, you could choose one of the restaurants overlooking the illuminated Rocca, or **Al Volt**, see ❷, north of Piazza 3 Novembre. Alternatively, the **Restel de Fer** (see page 119), between Riva and Torbole, is well worth the walk (1.6km/1 mile) or short drive from the centre.

MILAN

The dynamic business and design capital of Italy presents the perfect urban antidote to the languid atmosphere of the lakes. On this day excursion, explore the Duomo, indulge in designer shopping and stroll by night in the arty Brera quarter or lively Navigli.

DISTANCE: Minimum 3km (2 miles) on foot
TIME: A full day
START: Piazza del Duomo
END: Brera quarter
POINTS TO NOTE: From Como, Stresa, Bergamo or Varese, a direct train journey takes about an hour. From the Stazione Centrale, Milan's main rail station, catch the metro to the Duomo (cathedral). Consider booking a night at the opera (tel: Infotel Scala 02-7200 3744 or book online at www.teatroallascala.org). A viewing of *The Last Supper* should also be booked well in advance (see page 100).

The lure of Milan for most visitors is the chance to indulge in designer shopping in Italy's fashion citadel. Further temptation comes in the form of culture on an international scale, from the Duomo to opera at La Scala to Leonardo's *The Last Supper*. The historic city centre is easily manageable for visitors, and the dis-tances between the cathedral and the designer shopping district are walka-ble.

THE DUOMO

Piazza del Duomo is dominated by Europe's largest Gothic cathedral, the **Duomo** ❶ (www.duomomilano. it; Cathedral open daily 8am–7pm, rooftops every day 9am–7pm, last ticket 6pm; charge. The Crypt of Saint Charles Mon–Fri 11am–5.30pm, Sat 11am–5pm, Sun 1.30–3.30pm; free). The capacity is around 40,000 people, and the façade is adorned by 3,000 statues, 135 spires and 96 gar-goyles. This unfinished masterpiece was begun in 1386, and seamlessly blends Gothic, Baroque, neoclassical and neo-Gothic styles. French-style flying buttresses and soaring pinna-cles contrast with the excessive width preferred by native builders. Make a point of going up to the **terrazzi** (roof terraces), either by lift or (slightly cheaper) by clambering up 158 steps. For access to both, go to the back of

'The Last Supper' by Leonardo da Vinci

the Duomo. Apart from fine views of the city and, on very clear days, as far as the Matterhorn, you can admire the gilded figure of the sacred **Madonnina**, the city's protector, soaring over Gothic spires.

La Rinascente

Just off the square, **La Rinascente** (Via Santa Radegonda 3), the city's most upmarket department store, makes a possible first port of call for shopping. Its panoramic rooftop restaurant, **Le Terrazze**, overlooks the spires of the

cathedral. If food shopping is on the agenda, then head for **Peck** (Via Spadari 9), a gastronomic temple west of the cathedral.

GALLERIA VITTORIO EMANUELE II

Connecting Piazza del Duomo with La Scala opera house is the **Galleria Vittorio Emanuele II ❷**, a splendidly arcaded shopping gallery and rendezvous known as *il salotto di Milano* (Milan's front parlour).

Among the restaurant/bars here, **Savini** (tel: 02-7200 3433) has been welcoming stars from La Scala since 1867. This is the place for Lombard classics, but its formality can be oppressive. Among the Galleria's best bars is the Art Nouveau **Zucca in Galleria** at no. 78 (the Duomo end). It is a classic spot for an *aperitivo* – especially a Campari, as Davide Campari, the inventor of the drink, was born here on the first floor. Other perfect people-watching spots include café/restaurant **Biffi** (tel: 02-805 7961) and Marchesi 1824, which serves delicious snacks, pastries, and coffees.

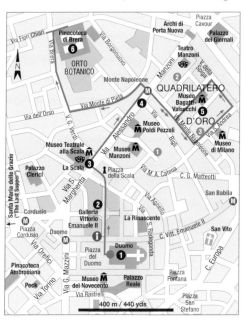

Galleria Vittorio Emanuele II

LA SCALA

The Galleria leads to Piazza della Scala, home to **La Scala ❸**, Italy's most celebrated opera house, which reopened at the end of 2004 after a lengthy, and controversial, refurbishment. A visit to the **Museo Teatrale alla Scala** (daily 9am–5.30pm; final admission 5pm; charge), which traces the history of opera and theatre in the city, allows you to peep into the fabulously opulent interior.

Museo PoldiPezzoli

You won't have time for many museums on a day trip to Milan, but this one is a real gem – and not too big. You will pass it en route from La Scala to the fashion shopping district. The **Museo Poldi Pezzoli** (Via Manzoni 12; www.museopoldipezzoli.it; Wed–Mon 10am–6pm; charge) contains an exquisite collection of Renaissance paintings, antiques and curios that belonged to Gian Giacomo Poldi Pezzoli, who owned the palace in the 19th century. On his death he stipulated that the building and contents should be accessible to the public.

QUADRILATERO D'ORO

From Piazza della Scala, head northeast along **Via Manzoni ❹** towards the world-famous shoppping quarter. If it's time for lunch and you want to follow in the footsteps of Verdi, Donizetti and Toscanini, divert to the **Antico Ristorante Boeucc**, see ❶, by taking the first turn on the right, leading to Piazza Belgioioso. Another Milanese institution is **Bice**, see ❷, further on, in the heart of the fashion district.

The so-called **Quadrilatero d'Oro ❺** (Golden Quadrangle) is defined by Via Manzoni, Via Monte Napoleone, Via della Spiga and Via Sant'Andrea, home to all the big fashion designers. At the intersection of Via Monte Napoleone and Via Sant'Andrea, call in at the **Pasticceria Cova**, see ❸, one of the few family shops that have survived the ever-increasing rents in the quarter.

After a reviving coffee, cross over Via Manzoni for Via Monte di Pietà and take the second street on the right for **Via Brera**.

THE BRERA

Formerly the city's artisan district, this is a chic, picturesque area, with

---

The Last Supper

Somewhat out on a limb geographically, Milan's single most famous sight is Leonardo da Vinci's exquisite painting of *The Last Supper*, know to the Italians as Il Cenacolo. It 'hangs' on the refectory wall of the church of Santa Maria delle Grazie (Piazza Santa Maria delle Grazie 2; tel: 02-9280 0360; www.vivaticket.it; Tue–Sun 8.15am–6.45pm; charge). Book well ahead to guarantee a viewing slot. Just 30 visitors are allowed in at any one time, and the visit is limited to 15 minutes.

Italy's fashion capital   *Duomo roof terraces*

art galleries and alternative bars still providing a colourful hint of the bohemian.

Brera Art Gallery

The quarter is home to Milan's showcase museum, the **Pinacoteca di Brera ❻** (Brera Art Gallery; Via Brera 28; pinacotecabrera.org; Tue–Sun 8.30am–7.15pm, last entry 6.40pm; charge), with one of the finest collections of Italian masterpieces. The collection spans some six centuries and includes works by Mantegna, Giovanni Bellini, Tintoretto, Veronese and Caravaggio.

Nightlife

If you decide to spend the evening in Milan, the liveliest streets in the centre are in the Brera – **Via Brera** and **Via Fiori Chiari**, both of which are popular for an evening stroll. Via Fiori Chiari fills with fortune tellers and illegal street traders selling fake designer goods as night falls. Alternatively, sample the nightlife of the trendy **Navigli** canal quarter, southwest of the centre (Porta Genova metro).

If you are enamoured of the fashion district, then slink into the bar at the Four Seasons Hotel (Via Gesù 6/8). Set in a frescoed former monastery, this is a glamorous place for an early evening *aperitif*.

Food and drink

❶ ANTICO RISTORANTE BOEUCC

Piazza Belgioioso 2; tel: 02-7602 0224; www.boeucc.it; Sun–Fri, Sun dinner only; €€€

The oldest restaurant in Milan, offering classic Milanese cuisine within a fabulous late-17th-century palazzo. Dishes such as *antipastino caldo del pescatore* (hot fish hors d'oeuvre based on a recipe given to the restaurant by Toscanini), saffron-flavoured *risotto alla milanese* and *costolettine di capretto con trevisana* (cutlets with radicchio) are served by smart waiters.

❷ BICE

Via Borgospesso 12; tel: 02 795528; www.bicemilano.it; closed Sunday evening; €€

This is *the* classic spot for Milanese risotto and celebrity-spotting, serving traditional gourmet cuisine in a bustling atmosphere. If the main menu, ending in a long list of creamy desserts, looks all too much, you can opt for one of the two-course light-lunch menus, with a glass of wine included. Vegetarian meals are available.

❸ PASTICCERIA COVA

Via Monte Napoleone 8; tel: 02-7600 5599; www.pasticceriacova.com; Mon–Sat 7.45am–8.30pm, Sun 9.30am–7.30pm; €

An elegant, historic *pasticceria/caffè*, ideal for a coffee-and-cake break while you are shopping in the Quadrilatero d'Oro. Specialities are *Sachertorte* (chocolate cake) and *panettone* (the light Milanese Christmas cake, nowadays eaten at any time of year).

DIRECTORY

Hand-picked hotels and restaurants to suit all budgets and tastes, organised by area, plus select nightlife listings, an alphabetical listing of practical information, a language guide and an overview of the best books and films to give you a flavour of the region.

The imposing Grand Hôtel des Iles Borromées

ACCOMMODATION

Accommodation on the lakes is abundant, with grand dowager hotels on the waterfront, romantic retreats in the hills, farmhouses, city-centre designer hotels, and self-catering villas and apartments. Accommodation is not cheap, especially if you choose a lakeside location. Hotels are categorised from one to five stars and five-star deluxe; the stars refer to facilities rather than quality.

Seasonal variations

Many of the lake hotels are closed between October and March. In high season (which varies according to hotel, but includes Easter and can go all the way from May through to September), hotels with a restaurant may insist on half-board with stays of no less than three days. Provided you know the hotel has a decent restaurant, half- (or full) board can be very good value.

Agriturismi

Working farms, converted barns or other rural properties that rent out rooms or apartments are known as *agriturismi*. These are an excellent choice for exploring rural regions, and for active holidays such as walking, fishing and cycling. Some *agriturismi* offer breakfast and an evening meal based on home-grown produce. Details of properties are available on www.agriturist.it and www.agriturismo.net.

Tourist tax

The Tassa di Soggiorno, a tourist tax reintroduced just a few years ago, may come as a nasty surprise at the end of your stay. The cost varies from region to region and depends on the star rating of the hotel. In Como for example you will be charged from €1 (1 star hotel) to €2.50 (4 star hotel) per person per night so a couple staying in a four star hotel for four nights would have to pay an extra €20. The tax is levied on a maximum number of nights, which can be anything from 4–10. Young children are usually excluded. If you have prepaid your hotel bill the tax will not have been included (or mentioned) – it is always charged when you check out at the hotel. B&Bs and residences are also included, usually at a slightly lower rate.

Price guide for a double room for one night with breakfast:
€€€€ = over 350 euros
€€€ = 200–350 euros
€€ = 130–200 euros
€ = below 130 euros

Lake Maggiore

Camin Hotel Colmegna
Via A. Palazzi 1, Luino; tel: 0332-510 855;
www.caminhotel.com; €€
A late-18th-century villa, built on a hunting estate and set in a large park with roman-

tic trails and a waterfall. Retaining its rustic charm, this family-run hotel has prettily decorated guest rooms, a restaurant specialising in lake fish and a private beach. Two terraces make the most of the lake views. Three suites are also available.

Grand Hotel des Iles Borromées & Spa

Corso Umberto I, 67, Stresa; tel: 0323-938 938; www.borromees.it; €€€€

Stresa's grande dame, this historic waterfront hotel faces the Borromean Islands. The *belle époque* decor is stylishly patrician, if somewhat ponderous. Many of the luxury rooms have fabulous views of the lake and Alps. Facilities include palm-shaded gardens, indoor and outdoor swimming pools, a spa and fitness centre, tennis courts, a helipad and a landing stage for private boats.

Grand Hotel Majestic

Via Vittorio Veneto 32, Verbania; tel: 0323-509 711; www.grandhotelmajestic.it; €€€

Another historic hotel, built in 1870, this great lady was favoured by artists from Debussy to Toscanini. Most rooms have panoramic views of the lake, while the wellness centre offers Ayurvedic and beauty treatments. There are lush gardens, a pool and small sandy beach too.

Hotel Garni Millennium

Via Dogana Nuova 2, tel: 091-759 6767; www.millennium-hotel.ch; €€

Once the town's customs house, today this handsome building is a small hotel with simply furnished rooms. Fully renovated in 2018; request a room with a lake view. Friendly, helpful staff.

Lido

Viale Libertà 11, Angera; tel: 0331-930 232; www.hotellido.it; €

An engaging villa-hotel with a private beach and good fish restaurant (see page 37). The guest rooms are peaceful and functional.

Pironi

Via Marconi 35, Cannobio; tel: 0323-70624; www.pironihotel.it; €€

A gem of a hotel, housed in a converted medieval Franciscan monastery. Original features, such as frescoes, vaulted ceilings and medieval columns, have been retained, and guest rooms are all individually furnished with antiques. The old cellars have been transformed into an inviting wine bar.

Il Porticciolo

Via Fortino 40, Laveno; tel: 0332-667 257; www.ilporticciolo.com; €€

A scenic four-star hotel on the lake with views of the Alps across the water. The rooms are comfortable, and there is a fine panoramic fish restaurant that serves lake fish, trout ravioli and scampi risotto.

Il Sole di Ranco

Piazza Venezia 5, Ranco; tel: 0331-976 507; www.ilsolediranco.it; €€€

Situated 4km (2.5 miles) north of Angera, this peaceful family-run four-

The view from Villa Aminta

star villa-hotel has a graceful, restful style, lush grounds and lakeside views. Although the emphasis here is on the gourmet restaurant (see page 113), the hotel has 14 rooms, including luxury suites with lake views. A swimming pool and sauna add to the attractions of this long-established inn.

Villa Aminta

Via Sempione Nord 123, Stresa; tel: 0323-933 818; www.villa-aminta.it; €€€€

This ravishing little Art Nouveau hotel was built by an Italian admiral in 1918; it now belongs to The Leading Small Hotels of the World chain. Gourmet fare (see page 113), a spa and fitness centre and views overlooking the pool and lake are all found here.

Lake Orta

La Bussola

Via Panoramica 24; tel: 0322-911 913; www.hotelbussolaorta.it; €€

Set in an elevated position, this welcoming family-run hotel has stupendous views over the lake and across to the Isola San Giulio. The rooms are charming, and the superior rooms have views of the lake. There is an outdoor swimming pool in the gardens and a panoramic terrace restaurant. On-site parking. Closed in November.

Hotel Aracoeli

Piazza Motta 34; tel: 0322-905 173; www.orta.net/aracoeli; €€

This very central little hotel is minimalist and quirky. Each of the seven rooms is individually designed – with futons, waterfall showers with transparent walls and breath-taking views of the lake. Very good breakfasts. There is parking up the hill. Can be closed late autumn and winter Closed. Call for the specific dates.

Hotel Cortese

Via Due Riviere 24C; tel: 0322-999 081; www.cortesehotel.it; €€

Standing at the foot of Monte Mottarone, this 4-star hotel has spectacular views of the surrounding hills, woodland and the lake. Rooms are well equipped and of a good size. There is an open-air swimming pool. Hotel is closed for the winter time.

Leon d'Oro

Piazza Motta, Orta San Giulio; tel: 0332-911 991; www.albergoleondoro.it; €

A family-run hotel with a romantic setting on the waterfront, overlooking the island of San Giulio. The standard bedrooms are small but bright and airy, many with good views. See page 51 for information on its restaurant.

Villa Crespi

Via G. Fava 18, Orta San Giulio; tel: 0322-911 902; www.villacrespi.it; €€€€

This grandiose Moorish folly has atmospheric public rooms as well as personalised bedrooms with canopied beds and whirlpool baths. The *raison d'être* here

The spa at Villa Aminta   *A luxury suite at Villa Aminta*

is the lovely two-Michelin-starred restaurant with sophisticated cuisine (see page 114).

Varese

Art Hotel
Via Bertini 3, Viale Aguggiari 26; tel: 0332-214 000; www.arthotelvarese.it; €€€
Charmingly converted into a small hotel, this Biumo palazzo, at the foot of the Sacro Monte, within easy walking distance of the city centre, has a lovely garden, bar and sitting room. The rooms are simply but stylishly furnished (shower but no bath). Breakfast is excellent, and the small restaurant makes good use of local ingredients. Highly recommended.

Hotel di Varese
Via Como 12; tel: 0332-237 559; www.hoteldivarese.it; €€
This hotel in Varese's historic centre is set in a beautiful Liberty villa that has been impeccably restored. Its 21 rooms are furnished in modern style, with clean lines and soothing colours. A generous breakfast is taken in the attractive breakfast room or in the garden.

Palace Grand Hotel Varese
Via L. Manara 11, Varese; tel: 0332-327 100; www.palacevarese.com; €€€
This is Varese's top hotel – an Art Nouveau palace set on Mont Campigli, with gorgeous views across the city, lake and hills. The public rooms have a ponderous charm, while suites are spacious. Guests have included Bob Dylan and Catherine Deneuve. There is a haute-cuisine restaurant here, plus gardens, tennis courts, a swimming pool and gym.

Sunset Hotel
Via al Lido 7, 21026 Gavirate; tel: 0332-731 023; www.sunsethotel.it; €€
On the lake shore at the north end of Lake Varese, this isn't the most beautiful hotel on earth, its 52 rooms rather boxy in shape and the sunset colours more like bacon and eggs. But the rooms are comfortable and well furnished with balconies and lake views, while the open-air pool is joined by a full spa complex with hydro massage and other ways to spoil yourself. And there's the sunset.

Lake Como

Bellavista
Piazza Bonacossa 2, Brunate; tel: 031-221 031; www.bellavistabrunate.com; €€
Reopened in 2013 after a revamp, this hotel in the hilltop village of Brunate lives up to its name and has stupendous views of Como and the Alps. An Art Nouveau boutique hotel, it is a peaceful spot, with a panoramic restaurant, garden and wellness area; the funicular down to Como is just 50 metres away. At the lower end of this price range.

Le Due Corti
Piazza Vittoria 12/13, Como; tel: 031-328 111; www.hotelduecorti.it; €€€
This former monastery and post house has been sensitively converted, despite the pool being placed in what were

A suite with a view at Grand Hotel Tremezzo

once the cloisters. The mood is one of quiet good taste, with warm fabrics and exposed beams matched by cosy rooms and a good restaurant.

Florence

Piazza Mazzini 46, Bellagio; tel: 031-950 342; www.hotelflorencebellagio.it; €€€

A charming traditional hotel that has been in the same family for over 160 years. Public rooms feature a mix of burnished wood panelling and contemporary furniture; bedrooms are warmly inviting and priced according to views. There is a good restaurant, a bar with a lakeside terrace and a small spa.

Grand Hotel Menaggio

Via IV Novembre 77, Menaggio; tel: 0344-30640; www.grandhotelmenaggio.com; €€

A four-star lakeside hotel with panoramic views and well-equipped bedrooms. The service is good, and facilities include two restaurants, a terrace, bar, heated pool, gardens, private moorings for boats, water-skiing equipment and parking.

Grand Hotel Tremezzo

Via Regina 8, Tremezzo; tel: 0344-42491; www.grandhoteltremezzo.com; €€€€

Close to Villa Carlotta on the western shore, this is one of the lake's finest hotels. Built in 1910, it is furnished in Art Nouveau style, and offers tasteful period rooms and terraced grounds dotted with modern sculptures. Facilities include five restaurants and bars, three

swimming pools (one with a breath-taking view of the lake), a spa, yoga studio, private beach and marina.

Villa d'Este

Via Regina 40, Cernobbio; tel: 031-3481; www.villadeste.it; €€€€

The undisputed empress of the lake, this sumptuous 16th-century villa has been a hotel since 1873 and features palatial frescoed rooms studded with antiques. Fans praise the professionalism, critics complain of the coldness. Facilities abound, with a luxury spa, nightclub, lake-floating pool, indoor pool, golf, watersports, eight tennis courts, squash courts, a gym, sauna and Turkish bath. This has long been a retreat for the rich and famous, from J.F. Kennedy to Alfred Hitchcock to Madonna. Caroline of Brunswick lived here for five years.

Grand Hotel Villa Serbelloni

Via Roma 1, Bellagio; tel: 031-950 216; www.villaserbelloni.com; €€€€

A luxury hotel comparable with Villa d'Este, with a wealth of marble, crystal chandeliers and frescos. With two restaurants (one Michelin-starred), three bars, a state-of-the-art health spa, outdoor pool, private beach, watersports and tennis, it has everything you could want, plus superb lake views.

Locanda Sant'Anna

Via Per Schignano, Argegno (Como); tel: 031-821 738; www.locandasantanna.it; €

The palatial bar at Villa d'Este   *Villa d'Este, the empress of the lake*

A rural retreat in the hills above Argegno, this family-run inn was once a retreat for Como clergy. There are eight comfortable rustic rooms, one suite and a recommended restaurant (see page 115).

Bergamo

B&B La Torre della Meridiana

Via Gombito 17a, Bergamo; tel: 335-207 659; www.latorredellameridiana.com; €

Right in the heart of Città Alta, historical centre of Bergamo, and near the cable-car and the old square, this B&B offers two bedrooms with a shared bathroom on the 4th floor of the ancient house. Located along the main street that passes through the whole historical centre.

Gombit Hotel

Via Mario Lupo 6, tel: 035-247 009; www.gombithotel.com; €€

Next to the medieval Torre del Gombito, this was the first designer hotel in the upper town. Modern and stylish, the 13 guest rooms are individually decorated, typically with exposed brick stonework or timbers and pastel-coloured furnishings.

Petronilla Hotel

Via San Lazzaro 4; tel: 035-271 376; www.petronillahotel.com; €€€

Behind a stately façade right in the heart of the city, the interior of this intimate 12-room boutique hotel surprises with its vibrant modern interior featuring bright canvases on the walls, cool designer furnishings and zesty pops of colour. Service is top-notch; prepare to be pampered.

Lake Iseo

Araba Fenice

Via Caproni 246, Località Pilzone d'Iseo, (2.8km/1.75 miles northeast of Iseo); tel: 030-982 2004; www.arabafenicehotel.it; €€

A good-value four-star hotel, with fabulous lake views and an excellent restaurant that serves Lombard cuisine and fish specialities, and decent breakfasts too. Nearly all the 34 rooms have views, and there is a sunny terrace for meals or drinks in fine weather.

Riva Lago

Via Cadorna 7, Sulzano; tel: 030 985 011; www.rivalago.it; €€

This elegant hotel with a pale blue classical façade enjoys an idyllic setting right on the lake, just a ferry hop away from the island of Monte Isola. Guest rooms are cream-coloured, light and airy, breakfasts are lavish affairs by the lakeside, the pool is a comfortable 29 degrees and the bar offers delicious Franciacorta sparkling wines by the glass.

Franciacorta

L'Albereta

Via Vittorio Emanuele II, Erbusco; tel: 030-776 0550; www.albereta.it; €€€€

A villa hotel that once showcased the skills of well-known chef, Gualtiero Marchesi now presents Chef Fabio Abbattista overseeing its kitchen following the former's death. Set in Franciacorta wine country, it is marble-studded and gilded, exuding a spurious glamour. A favourite among those with limitless pockets and gourmet

The lakeside restaurant at Villa Fiordaliso

tastes. As well as a pool, tennis and spa centre, wine-tasting trips are available.

Azienda Agricola

Al Rocol, Via Provinciale 79, Ome; tel: 030-685 2542; www.alrocol.com; €

Wine estate and farm with simple but tasteful bedrooms and apartments on a family-run estate producing award-winning Franciacorta wines, olive oil, honey and grappa.

Cappuccini Convento

Via Cappuccini 54, Cologne Franciacorta; tel: 030-715 7254; www.cappuccini.it and www.franciacorta.net; €€

Set on a hilltop overlooking Franciacorta, this 16th-century former monastery is now a gracious inn, restaurant and small spa – although walking the lovely grounds is equally therapeutic. Wine-tasting, elegant restaurant (with old regional recipes using fresh produce from the monastic orchards and vegetable gardens), old-world bedrooms and 'wine therapy' in the spa.

Relais Franciacorta

Via Manzoni 29, Colombaro (Franciacorta); tel: 030-988 4234; www.relaisfranciacorta.it; €€

Popular 17th-century farm estate converted into elegant rural hotel. It's a peaceful spot with large grounds and views towards Lake Iseo. Inside, the bedrooms are spacious, and there are two different restaurants. Activities include wine-tasting, biking, horseback riding.

Lake Garda

Color Hotel

Via Santa Cristina 5; tel: 045-621 0857; www.colorhotel.it; €€€

The fresh, modern design of this hotel makes interesting use of colour and light. The rooms are spacious with balconies, a variety of bars and lounges and there are several pools in the gorgeous gardens. Bicycles and mountain bikes can be borrowed free of charge. Closed mid autumn and winter.

Gardesana

Piazza Calderini 5, Torri del Benaco; tel: 045-722 5411; gardesana.eu; €€

Given it has hosted the likes of Churchill, Laurence Olivier, Maria Callas and King Juan Carlos I of Spain, this traditional hotel is delightfully low-key, and the Venetian-style rooms are well priced. The harbour side setting is enchanting. Well rated restaurant with a gorgeous setting.

Grand Hotel Fasano

Corso Zanardelli, 190, Gardone Riviera; tel: 0365-290 220; www.ghf.it; €€€€

Once a hunting lodge, this opulent five-star hotel has lush grounds and old-world grandeur. Luxurious guest rooms vary in size and are priced accordingly. Along with gourmet cuisine, there is a stylish spa, indoor pool and private lakeside beach.

Laurin

Viale Landi 9, Salò; tel: 0365-22022; hotellaurinsalo.it; €€€

Breakfast terrace at Laurin

The view from a Laurin suite

This sumptuous Art Nouveau villa, set in gorgeous lake-view grounds, served as the Ministry of Foreign Affairs during Mussolini's puppet regime. A fine restaurant is the setting for high-class cuisine. Rooms were recently refurbished by the artist Rivadossi.

Locanda San Vigilio

Punta San Vigilio; tel: 045-725 6688; www. locanda-sanvigilio.it; €€€€

With one of the most beautiful settings on the lake, this tiny hotel has only seven rooms, four superior rooms and three suites; specify if you want a lake view, as not all have balconies. It also has one of the best restaurants in the region, where you can dine alfresco in a perfect romantic setting. For extra privacy, ask for the Limonaia, reached through Italy's oldest lemon grove. Arrive by boat or helicopter for added panache. Booking advised.

Le Palme

Via Porto 36, Limone sul Garda; tel: 0365-954 4681; www.sunhotels.it; €€

Set beside the ferry landing stage, this 17th-century waterfront hotel is in a quaint but touristy resort. It has a small pool, a rooftop sun terrace, a restaurant, a la carte menu, a bar with live music and a panoramic whirlpool.

Villa Cortine Palace Hotel

Viale C. Gennari 2, Sirmione; tel: 030-990 5890; www.palacehotelvillacortine.com; €€€€

A romantic luxury hotel set in parkland a few minutes' walk from the crowds of Sir-

mione's historic centre. The neoclassical villa has landscaped gardens with fountains, a pool, tennis courts, watersports, a private jetty with boats to rent and a path to a beach restaurant. w

Villa Fiordaliso

Corso Zanardelli 132, Gardone Riviera; tel: 0365-20158; www.villafiordaliso.com; €€€€

An exclusive Art Nouveau villa hotel where Mussolini and Clara Petacci once stayed. It has a beautiful lakeside setting and a richly decorated interior, but the real highlight is the restaurant with waterside terrace (see page 120).

Milan

Antica Locanda Leonardo

Corso Magenta 78, tel: 02-4801 4197; www. anticalocandaleonardo.com; €€

A stylishly restored, idiosyncratic hotel with an inner courtyard and garden. Popular with the fashion crowd.

Antica Locanda dei Mercanti

Via San Tomaso 8, tel: 02-805 4080; www. locanda.it; €€€

This charming boutique hotel has the cosiness of an old-fashioned inn. Some rooms have rooftop views.

Bulgari Hotel

Via Privata Fratelli Gabba 7B; tel: 02-805 8051; www.bulgarihotels.com; €€€€

On the edge of the Botanical Gardens, the Bulgari Hotel has been designed with the precision and opulence that is the trademark of the name. Eye-watering prices.

The aperitif is served at Villa Aminta

RESTAURANTS

Introduction

This upmarket part of Italy has more than its fair share of restaurants, from tiny, intimate spots to a cluster of grand Michelin-starred affairs, so you will certainly not be short of a place to eat. Many ingredients are locally sourced, with excellent lake fish. The most difficult part is simply deciding where to dine. Opening times are generally lunch *(pranzo)* 12/12.30pm–2/3pm and dinner *(cena)* 7.30/8pm–10pm. In main towns and resorts, restaurants may stay open later – this is often the case with pizzerias. Menus at lunchtime are frequently cheaper and lighter than those offered in the evening.

Lake Maggiore

Grotto Sant'Anna

Via Sant'Anna 30, Cannobio; tel: 0323-70682; Tue–Sun; €€
Along the Cannobina Valley, in the mountains behind Cannobio, this restaurant perches on the edge of a spectacular gorge. The simple menu features delicious meat dishes, excellent pasta, cheeses and home-made desserts. The restaurant is about 10km (6 miles) from Cannobio, and you can hike, bike or go by car.

Luina

Via Garibaldi 21, Stresa; tel: 0323-30285; Mar–Oct; €
Simple, friendly and good-value restaurant belonging to the Luina Hotel, halfway between the central piazza and the lake. Favourites here are the *cannelloni al forno* and the speciality risotto, which is made to order and well worth the wait. There is a terrace for summer dining.

Milano

Corso Zannitello 2, Pallanza; tel: 0323-556 816; lunch and dinner Wed–Mon, closed Nov–Mar; €€€
Feast on fresh fish such as perch and home-grown vegetables from the terrace overlooking the lake. The home-made pasta is wonderful, especially during truffle season.

Osteria del Centenario

Viale Verbano 17, Locarno; tel: 00 41-0-91 743 8222; osteriacentenario.ch; Tue–Sat; €€€
One of Locarno's best restaurants, with traditional Ticino architecture. Fresh

> Price guide for a two-course à la carte dinner for one with half a bottle of house wine:
> €€€€ = over 65 euros
> €€€ = 45–65 euros
> €€ = 25–45 euros
> € = below 25 euros

local ingredients are used to create dishes such as lobster salad, foie gras and stuffed lamb with asparagus.

Il Piccolo Lago

Via Filippo Turati 87, Verbania Fondotoce, Lago di Mergozzo; tel: 0323-586 792; www.piccololago.it; every night Wed–Sun, lunch Thu–Sun, closed Mon, late autumn and winter open only for private events; €€€
On the lakeshore road in Mergozzo, this is a top-class two-Michelin-starred restaurant with fabulous lake views. Intriguing menu created by chef Marco Sacco. A lovely unpretentious interior complements the views.

Ristorante Il Vicoletto

Vicolo del Poncivo 3; tel: 0323-932 102; www.ristorantevicoletto.com, lunch and dinner Fri–Wed; €€
This charming little family-run restaurant serves up imaginative, well presented dishes – try the tasty mussels and salmon curry. Due to its small size, booking is essential, particularly if you want to eat at one of the handful of outside tables.

Lo Scalo

Piazza Vittorio Emanuele III 32, Cannobio; tel: 0323-71480; www.loscalo.com; open every day from Apr 30th to Sept for lunch and dinner; €€€
This ancient arcaded palazzo, which used to shelter fishing boats, has a large terrace for summer lake-view dining. The elegant restaurant is known for first-class, sophisticated cuisine, featuring delicious home-made pastas and fish from the lake, as well as meat dishes.

Il Sole di Ranco

Piazza Venezia 5, Ranco; tel: 0331-976 507; www.ilsolediranco.it; closed Tue (except in high season); €€€€
Founded in 1850 by the Brovelli family, the restaurant is now run by the expert Davide who managed to mix tradition and modernity while respecting traditional customs. The award-winning restaurant sits right on the lake, with an arbour for summer dining. Dishes are elegantly presented and served. It is also a hotel with 14 rooms.

Il Vicoletto

Vicolo del Poncivo 3, Stresa; tel: 0323 932102; www.ristorantevicoletto.com; closed Thu Nov–Mar, may be closed off-season; €€
Tucked away in an alley off the main square this tiny restaurant with its contemporary menu bucks the trend of Stresa's pizzeria and spag-bol-orientated eateries. Expect simple pastas and roast meat and fish, using top-quality ingredients.

Villa Aminta

Via Sempione Nord 123, Stresa; tel: 0323-933 818; www.villa-aminta.it; Apr–Nov; €€€€
This villa is a delightful five-star luxury hotel with two alluring restau-

Expect molecular cuisine at Mistral

rants: the large richly decorated Le Isole with a candlelit terrace, which serves light lunches and gourmet set-menu dinners, and the enchanting a la carte Restaurant Mori. Both have gorgeous lake views, encompassing the Borromean Islands, and are justifiably sought after for weddings and private parties.

Lake Orta

Al Boeuc

Via Bersani 28, Orta San Giulio; tel: 0339 584 0039; Fri–Wed, €

Sample a good glass of wine or two accompanied by prosciutto, cheese or *bagna cauda* (crudités in hot olive oil, garlic and anchovy dip). This is the oldest and one of the most atmospheric taverns in town.

Al Sorriso

Via Roma 18, Soriso; tel: 0322-983 228; www.alsorriso.com; Wed–Sun, closed Jan; €€€€

This gastronomic Mecca in the tiny village of Soriso, 8km (5 miles) south of Orta San Giulio, attracts devotees from all over Europe. It may have lost one of its three Michelin stars but Piedmont and Mediterranean cuisine, produced by chef Luisa Valazza, is still inspirational. This is a family-run affair, with an elegant, friendly atmosphere (*sorriso* means 'smile'), but be prepared for arm-and-a-leg category prices. There are also eight comfy guest rooms should you choose to stay.

Villa Crespi

Via G. Fava 8/10, Orta San Giulio; tel: 0322-911 902; www.hotelvillacrespi.it; closed Tue off-season; €€€

An imaginative blend of Alpine and Mediterranean flavours, presented in the sumptuous surroundings of a Moorish-style villa that is now a hotel with this wonderful restaurant. Feast on Sicilian scampi, carnaroli rice with clams and thyme, Piedmont veal, sea bass with oysters and caviar – washed down with one of over 1,000 Italian and French wines. Two Michelin stars.

Lake Varese

Vecchia Riva

Via G. Macchi 146, Schiranna, Lago di Varese; tel: 0332-329 300/335; www.vecchiariva.com; closed on Wed; €€

Choose a fine day and sit in the garden, looking out onto the peaceful waters of Lake Varese. The restaurant serves up a fine spread of *antipasti* (where you can help yourself buffet-style), good fish, risotto and pasta dishes. It is also a hotel with functional modern rooms.

Lake Como

Acquadolce

Via Regina Vecchia 36, Carate Urio; tel: 031-400 260; www.ristoranteacquadolce.it; Wed–Sun; closed in Jan and Feb; €€€

This place enjoys a stylish modern setting right on the lake, sporting an enticing waterfront terrace. Home-made pasta, lake fish, salads and

The lake view at Mistral

A luxurious carpaccio at Mistral

decadent desserts are elegantly presented and served.

Il Cavatappi

Via XX Settembre, Varenna; tel: 0341-815 349; www.cavatappivarenna.it; Thu–Tue; €

'The Corkscrew' is a minute eatery, with just five tables, hidden in an alley off the main piazza of Varenna. The cuisine is simple but delicious, the atmosphere cosy and the wine cellar well stocked. Wines are used in certain dishes; menu offers vegetarian dishes. The owner-cum-chef will talk you through the local lake specialities. Booking advisable.

Il Gatto Nero

Via Montesanto 69, Cernobbio; tel: 031-512 042; open every day for lunch and dinner; www.ristorantegattonero.it; €€€€

Rub shoulders with celebrities (this is one of George Clooney's favourites), gaze down on to great lake views, and feast on fish and meat specialities. The 'Black Cat', perched in the hills above Cernobbio, is sumptuously decorated and has soft, mellow lighting and a romantic atmosphere. The food may not be quite all it is cracked up to be, but the setting alone is worth a detour.

Locanda Sant'Anna

Via Sant'Anna 152 (on the Schignano road), Argegno; tel: 031-821 738; www.locandasantanna.it; open daily for lunch and dinner; €€

A rural retreat in the hills above Argegno. Local dishes such as home-made tortel-

lini, potatoes and mushrooms soufflé, lamb, venison, grilled beef, salami and Alpine cheeses are served in two adjacent rooms, with a garden setting, and valley and lake views.

Mistral

Grand Hotel Villa Serbelloni, Via Roma 1; tel: 031-950 216; www.villaserbelloni.com; €€€

The Michelin-starred restaurant of this grand hotel produces 'molecular cuisine' (think ice creams cooled by liquid nitrogen and turbot cooked in melted sugars) along with Mediterranean specialities. Eat in a wood-panelled restaurant, evocative of the great lake steamers, or on the lakeside veranda.

Teatro

Piazza Verdi 11, Como; tel: 031-414 0363; ristorantecaffeteatro.it; Tue–Sun; €

In the heart of Como, on a piazza facing the Duomo, this is a stylish café and bistro in the same building as the historic Sociale Theatre. The café is open all day and evening, the bistro, with simple contemporary cuisine, for lunch and dinner. Tables are laid out on the square for alfresco meals in summer.

Vecchia Varenna

Contrada Scoscesa 14, Varenna; tel: 0341-830 793; www.vecchiavarenna.it; open daily for lunch and dinner; €€€

Managed by the Castiglioni family since 1987, restaurant Vecchia Varenna, is located in the historic part of town.

Le Grill, Villa d'Este

Amid an irresistible waterside setting, with Lake Como and mountain views, Vecchia Varenna serves fish and meat, pasta, rice meals and tasty desserts. Restaurant offers vegetarian and gluten free options.

Villa d'Este
Via Regina 40, Cernobbio; tel: 031-3481; www.villadeste.com; Grill, Il Platano and Terrazza Bar evenings only; €€€
Hotel Villa d'Este has three restaurants and three bars (one of which sports a club). The setting is a palatial 16th-century villa amid luxuriant gardens at Cernobbio. Formal Italian *haute cuisine* is served at the Veranda (jackets and ties are required in the evening), while The Grill, underneath the plane trees in summer, and Il Planto offers regional dishes in a more informal atmosphere.

Brescia region

Baretto di San Vigilio
Via Castello 1, San Vigilio, Bergamo; tel: 035-253 191; www.baretto.it; €€€€
At the top of Bergamo's San Vigilio funicular you can sit out on this romantic restaurant's terrace (in summer), enjoying gourmet fare and wonderful views of the Città Alta below. The menu offers a wide selection of home-made dishes. You might start with an *antipasti* or home-made pasta, follow with meat or fish, and finish off with one of their famous desserts. There are also 250 wines to choose from.

Cantina e Agriturismo Al Rocol
Via Provinciale 79, Ome, Franciacorta; tel: 030-685 2542; www.alrocol.com; €
This rustic inn is located on a family-run wine estate and farm. Brescian and Franciacorta dishes served here include *casonsèi* (ravioli with bacon and melted butter), tagliatelle with wild mushrooms, beef with local olive oil, and, in autumn and winter, *polenta e osei*, the 'Brescian lunch' of spit-roasted pork and chicken on polenta. Award-winning wines, olive oil, honey and grappa are all available to buy. Reservations essential.

Da Franco
Bartolomeo Colleoni 8, Bergamo; tel: 035-238 565; www.dafrancobergamo.org; Tue–Sun lunch and dinner; €
Located next to the beautiful and historical Piazza Vecchia, Da Franco is one of the best restaurants in the upper town. Good wine. Vegetarian, vegan and gluten free options.

Pizzeria La Bella Napoli
Via Taramelli 7, near Porta Nuova, Bergamo; tel: 035-242 308; €
Large and popular pizzeria in the Città Bassa (Lower Town) of Bergamo, catering for all tastes with over 200 types of pizza cooked in a traditional wood oven. Lively atmosphere and music at night.

Punta dell'Est
Via Ponta 163, Clusane; tel: 030-989 060;

The veranda at Villa d'Este is more formal

www.ristorantehotelpuntadellest.it; Tue–Sun; €€
The fish restaurant of this welcoming family-run hotel is the place to eat baked tench, the local speciality (baked eel is another). It has a wonderful setting right on the lake by the ferry landing stage.

Restaurant Hostaria

Piazza Mascheroni, 9a; tel: 035-237 383; www.relaisanlorenzo.com; Tue–Sat; €€€
An incomparable setting for an unforgettable experience. This gourmet restaurant of the Relais San Lorenzo hotel is embedded within a Roman and medieval archaeological site. The fine and varied cuisine will allow you to taste the pleasure of Italian dishes and valuable local products.

Relais I due Roccoli

Via Silvio Bonomelli, Loc. Invino di Sotto, Iseo, tel: 030-982 2977; www.idueroccoli. com; Apr–Oct; €€
This romantic hilltop eyrie above Iseo is a great place for truffles, fresh lake fish, mushroom dishes and chocolate desserts. The dining room has views over the lake, and there is a courtyard for summer dining by candlelight. Also a hotel.

Relais Mirabella

Via Mirabella 38, Clusane; tel: 030-989 8051; www.relaismirabella.it; Apr–Oct; €€
Located high up, 1.5km (1 mile) southwest of the centre of Clusane, with a lovely romantic terrace, this oasis of peace and elegance has wonderful views over the lake. Creative cuisine, including locally sourced fish, is presented with a flourish.

Restaurant LeoneFelice

L'Albereta Hotel, Via Vittorio Emanuele 23, Erbusco; tel: 030-776 2603; www.albereta. it; Tue–Sat; €€€
LeoneFelice is a sublime restaurant with a modern Italian design. The kitchen of Fabio Abbattista - the executive chef – offers a menu made with excellent ingredients. All meals are accompanied by great wines, mainly from the finest Franciacorta estates. Booking is essential.

Trattoria del Muliner

Via San Rocco 16, Clusane, tel: 030-982 9206; closed Tue; www.trattoriadelmuliner. it; €€
Clusane on Lake Iseo is famous for *tinca al forno* (baked tench) and this inviting, family-run trattoria is one of the best places to try it.

La Vineria

Via X Giorante 4, Brescia; tel: 030-280 543; closed Mon, Tue only lunch; www. lavineriabrescia.it; €
An authentic wine bar and inn in the town of Brescia, where you can sample excellent cold cuts and cheeses as well as hot dishes. Informal but informed tasting advice is offered on good regional wines.

Agriturismo Trenta

Via Mazzane 2, Moniga del Garda; tel: 0365-503 395; www.agriturismo30.com; opening hours vary by season; €€

A delightful *agriturismo* with a vine-covered terrace that overlooks the herb gardens and lake. The table d'hôte food is delicious, plentiful and affordable. Many of the ingredients, including fruit and wheat flour, are produced on the farm. Booking essential.

Caffè Italia

Piazza Malvezzi 19, Desenzano del Garda; tel: 030-914 1243; open daily; www.ristorantecaffeitalia.com; €€€

At this well-established café in the centre of the town you can enjoy anything from a morning cappuccino and croissant at the bar, a light lunch on the terrace, or a blow-out seven-course *menu degustazione* (tasting menu). The fish is utterly reliable, and includes French oysters, Sicilian scampi, sea bass and raw fish. This is also a fashionable spot for cocktails and liqueurs. Vegetarian friendly.

Esplanade

Via Lario 10, Desenzano del Garda; tel: 030-914 3361; www.ristorante-esplanade.com; Thu–Tue; €€€€

Outstanding cuisine and a panoramic lake setting combine to make this one of the most desirable restaurants in the region. Menu is seasonal and may include specialities like eel rolls with vegetables marinated in tarragon vinegar, sea bass ravioli with plankton broth and excellent desserts. There is a huge list of wines to choose from. Formal setting.

Gatto Moro

Via Giotto 21, Borghetto di Valeggio sul Mincio; tel: 045-637 0570; ristorantegattomoro.it; Wed–Mon; €€

An excellent restaurant with a long tradition. Gatto Moro serves traditional meals with only fresh ingredients. Menu was created by talented chef Flavio Rigatelli. Vegetarian friendly.

Pasticceria Vassalli

Via di San Carlo 84-6, Salò; tel: 0365-20752; www.pasticceria-vassalli.it; €

Specialising in chocolate, sweets and cakes, this café/*pasticceria* is hard to resist. Among the local favourites are *pan di Salò*, a rich cake made with candied peel and limoncello, a version of the liqueur made from Lake Garda lemons.

Il Porticciolo

Lungolago Marconi 22, Lazise; tel: 045-758 0254; www.ilporticcioloristorante.it; mid-Feb–mid-Dec; closed on Tue; €€

An inviting family-run lakeside restaurant that serves a vast array of fish and vegetable *antipasti*, and fresh fish such as grilled sea bass, risotto with tench and spaghetti "Carbonara of the Lake" (with fish).

Castel Toblino is an enchanting place to have a meal

Restel de Fer

Via Restel de Fer 10, Riva del Garda; tel: 0464-553 481; www.resteldefer.com; closed on Wed; €€€

Restel de Fer is a delightful rustic *locanda*, which has been run by the Meneghelli family since 1400. Try *trout carpaccio with fennel and elder* or marinated char salad.

Risorgimento

Piazza Carducci 5–6, Sirmione; tel: 030-916 325; Fri–Wed lunch and dinner, closed on Tue; may be closed off-season; www.risorgimento-sirmione.com; €€€

A centrally located restaurant, with tables on a piazza with views of the lake. Home-made pastas, seafood dishes, a selection of meats and mouth-watering desserts combine with excellent service. Very popular, so booking is advised.

Ristorante Castel Toblino

Sarche; tel: 0461-864 036; closed Mon and Tue, closed off-season; www.casteltoblino. com; €€€

A romantic castle on the enchanting Lake Toblino, offering three set menus (meat, lake fish and Trentino traditions) as well as a la carte. Snacks are available all day at the lakeside bar and there is a well-stocked wine cellar.

Ristorante Re Lear

Piazza Cavour 23, Malcesine; tel: 045-740 0616; €€€

Ranked as one of the top restaurants in Malcesine, the King Lear offers innovative combinations, such as thin octopus slices in Nori seaweed, rabbit fillet with asparagus polenta, and olive ice cream. Menus change monthly, and vegetarian, vegan and gluten free meals are available. The restaurant is in the heart of the Old Town, a stone's throw away from Castello Scaligero, with a terrace on Piazza Cavour.

La Rucola 2.0

Via Strentelle 3, Sirmione; tel: 030-916 326; Fri–Wed; www.ristorantelarucola.it; €€€

Recently renovated and redecorated, this is a Michelin star restaurant located close to the castle. The creative Mediterranean cuisine includes a wide choice of seafood and meat plus a huge wine selection with over 700 labels. Vegetarian options also available. Reservations are compulsory for dinner and advisable for lunch.

La Terrazza

Via Benaco 14, Torbole; tel: 0464-506 083; www.allaterrazza.com; opening hours vary by season; €€

The broad lake-view veranda and the inspired regional cuisine make this one of the most appealing restaurants in the northern part of Lake Garda. With ingredients sourced from the lake, specialities include chub meatballs, perch salad, lake sardines and risotto with tench. Wash your meal down with a

Milan's Navigli canal quarter

crisp Pinot Grigio or Muller Thurgau. Very good value.

La Tortuga

Via XXIV Maggio 5, Gargnano; tel: 036-571 251; www.ristorantelatortuga.it; opening hours vary by season; closed on Tue; €€€

This intimate little restaurant in the historic centre of Gargnano serves exquisite dishes and great wines. Fish (both lake and sea) predominate, but you can also find vegetarian *antipasti* and main courses, such as sea bass fillet with citrus marinated shrimp fennel cream, pigeon chest in Madeira sauce. Michelin-starred, with a well-stocked wine cellar.

Villa Feltrinelli

Via Rimembranze 38, Gargnano; tel: 0365-798 000; www.villafeltrinelli.com; Apr–Oct; €€€€

This lakeside retreat, built in 1892, was home to Mussolini during World War II, and today is a luxury hotel with rich period furnishings. The gourmet French-influenced restaurant is run by one of the region's best chefs.

Villa Fiordaliso

Corso Zanardelli 132, Gardone Riviera; tel: 0365-20158; www.villafiordaliso.com; €€€

This small and stylish Art Nouveau villa-hotel right on the lake is where Mussolini stayed with his mistress Clara Petacci during the Salò repub-lic. Stroll through the grounds after a gourmet lunch in the seductive Michelin-awarded restaurant.

Milan

El Brellin

Vicolo dei Lavandai, Alzaia Naviglio Grande 14; tel: 02-5810 1351; www.brellin.com; lunch and dinner daily; €€

Probably the most glamorous old washhouse ever. This 18th-century laundry, now an idyllic waterfront restaurant on the Naviglio Grande, has an evening menu of rich home-made pastas and Lombardy specialities such as creamy Milanese risotto. The locals love the Sunday brunch and happy-hour buffet.

Cracco

Via Victor Hugo 4; tel: 02-876774; www.ristorantecracco.it; Mon–Fri lunch and dinner, Sat dinner, closed on Sun; €€€€

Opened by the famous Italian chef Carlo Cracco, this gastronomic wonder was awarded one Michelin star for high-quality cooking. Specialities include fish soup crust and yolk marinated with asparagus and black truffle, saffron risotto and grilled bone marrow.

L'Anima Del Gusto

Via dei Fontanili 2; tel: 02 8954 6551; www.lanimadelgusto.eu; lunch and dinner Mon–Fri, Sat only dinner, Sun closed; €€

Restaurant offers a friendly atmosphere and delightful seafood dishes. Try tuna tartare with Bronte pistachios and avocado fragrance, tagliolini with red prawns and bottarga and grilled swordfish with fennel and orange salad. Somewhat off the beaten track – but worth the taxi fare.

Gelateria Marghera

Via Marghera 33, Fiera, tel: 02-468 641; www.gelateriamarghera.it; open daily; €

Join a queue that stretches round the block for the best ice cream in Milan. This gelateria has an overwhelming array of flavours to choose from – plus delicious semifreddi and meringue cakes. Heaven on a hot day and definitely worth the wait.

Joia

Via Panfilo Castaldi 18; tel: 02-295 22124; www.joia.it; Mon–Sat lunch and dinner, closed on Sun; €€€€

Atypical of meat-eating Milan, Joia specialises in vegetarian haute cuisine (as well as fish). The setting is simple and contemporary, the clientele hip, the presentation unique. The cuisine is avant-garde and capricious featuring dishes such as Bellevue artichoke cooked slowly in a crust with homemade traditional jam with leek and ginger – as a main course. The Michelin star means high prices, but the lunch menus are good value. Book at least one week ahead.

Luini

Via Santa Radegonda 16, tel: 02-8646 1917; www.luini.it; Mon 10am–3pm, Tue–Sat 10am–8pm; €

Very handy for a quick snack by the Duomo, this famous bakery specialises in *panzerotto*, a freshly made Puglian pastry folded over fillings of tomato and mozzarella, ricotta, ham and spinach. No credit cards.

Osteria di Porta Cicca

Ripa di Porta Ticinese 51; tel: 02-837 2763; www.osteriadiportacicca.it; Sat and Sun lunch and dinner, Tue–Fri dinner, Mon closed ; €€€

This softly lit, elegant restaurant in the Navigli district is perfect for a romantic meal. The menu offers a few carefully chosen dishes for each course, with interesting flavour combinations – follow the tagliatelle with duck ragout with a robust portion of hare with polenta. The Sunday brunch is popular with locals.

Trattoria Milanese

Via Santa Marta 11; tel: 02-8645 1991; Mon-Sat; €€

In the centre of Milan, this is one of a few remaining traditional *trattorie*. Since 1919, it has served simple Lombard fare in a warm, friendly atmosphere. Classic dishes are *osso buco* (braised veal shanks) served with polenta, *risotto alla milanese* and *cotoletta alla milanese* (breaded and fried veal). It also serves great seafood.

Lake Garda is the best equipped for families

A–Z

A

Age restrictions

The age limit for consuming and purchasing alcohol in Italy is 18, following a change in laws. Stricter penalties on establishments selling to those under 18 have been enacted. The age of consent is 14, but can be 16 in some cases. The minimum age for driving, provided you hold a full licence, is 18 but for renting a car in most cases a driver must be 21 or over.

B

Budgeting

The best-value hotels and restaurants tend to be located away from the lake fronts. In high season you can expect to pay €175–275 for a comfortable double room with bath, €100–150 in a simple hotel or B&B. Count on €40–65 upwards for a three-course evening meal with half a bottle of wine in a restaurant, and €18 or so for a pizza and beer. Drinks and coffee taken at the bar are quite a bit cheaper than those at a table with waiter service. Entrance fees to museums, galleries and gardens range from €2–13; entrance is free for EU citizens under 18 (but no longer for those over 65) and those from 18–25 normally get a 50 percent discount. Fuel costs are similar to those across Europe, but public transport remains comfortably inexpensive.

Business hours

Banks are generally open weekdays 8.30am–1.30pm and 3–4pm (afternoon opening times may vary). Banks at airports and main stations usually have longer opening hours and are open at weekends.

Shops are traditionally open from Monday–Saturday 9am–1pm and 3.30/4–7.30pm, but an increasing number of stores, especially in the cities, are open all day. Resorts such as Stresa and Bellagio notwithstanding, most shops are closed on Sunday, and some also close on Monday morning.

C

Children

There is plenty to keep youngsters entertained on the lakes, from boat trips and cable-car rides to leisure parks and castles. Lake Garda is by far the best-equipped lake for families, with vast theme parks, water parks, and sandy beaches. Concentrated in a 25km (15.5-mile) radius in the southeast of Lake Garda, there are a number of major attractions.

Lake Maggiore lights up at night

Villa Pallavicino

Lake Maggiore's Stresa may be a rather sedate resort, but children can be kept entertained by ferry rides, the Monte Mottarone cable-car, and a visit to Villa Pallavicino (www.parcopallavicino.it). The extensive gardens are home to animals, exotic birds and a children's playground. In summer, a mini-train provides a shuttle service between the park and Stresa's centre.

Theme parks

Thousands of holidaymakers descend annually to the shore north of Peschiera del Garda, home to Gardaland (www.gardaland.it), Italy's number one theme park. It boasts over 40 Disney-styled attractions and 40 shows.

Situated 4km (2.5 miles) to the north is CanevaWorld and its Movieland Studios (www.canevaworld.it), which comprises the fun-filled Acqua Water Park and film-themed attractions.

The most exciting rides in the region are the Monte Baldo cable-car (see page 89) where rotating panoramic pods ascend Monte Baldo and the new Alpyland (see page 39), a bob-sled roller coaster on Monte Mottarone, Lake Maggiore.

Water parks and gardens

The Parco Cavour near Valeggio sul Mincio (www.parcoacquaticocavour.it) provides plenty of aquatic entertainment. Nature lovers should head for the Parco Natura Viva at Bussolengo (www.parco-naturaviva.it), a centre for the protection of animals at risk of extinction. The Parco Giardino Sigurtà (www.sigurta.it) at Valeggio sul Mincio features aquatic gardens, with fish-filled ponds, a toy railway, and nature trails.

Climate

Spring, summer and autumn are all good times to visit the lakes, not least due to the fine weather conditions. Ideal months are May, June and September, when it is warm and sunny but not as hot as midsummer and not quite as crowded. April and May are the best months for the blooming of camellias, azaleas and tulips.

The climate can be unpredictable due to differences in altitude and microclimates. In Milan, temperatures can soar in summer to well above 30°C (86°F) and the humidity is high – hence the exodus of Milanese to the cooler lakes. October and November are the wettest months in the region but usually include quite a few unexpectedly fine days. Winter tends to be foggy and cold, and is best avoided.

Crime and safety

The lakeside resorts are generally very safe, as are most of the small towns. In Milan keep an eye on possessions, especially in crowded places such as the Piazza del Duomo and train and bus stations. For insurance purposes, theft and loss must be reported straight away

to the police station *(questura)*. In case of theft, take photocopies of flight tickets, driving licence, passport and insurance documents.

Customs

Free exchange of non-duty-free goods for personal use is allowed between EU countries. The following are the guidance levels:

Tobacco: 800 cigarettes, or 400 cigarillos, or 200 cigars, or 1kg of tobacco.
Spirits: 10 litres above 22% strength or 20 litres below 22% strength.
Wine: 90 litres (only 60 litres can be sparkling).
Beer: 110 litres.

Those from non-EU countries should refer to their home country's regulating organisation for a current complete list of import restrictions.

E

Electricity

Sockets take two-pin, round-pronged plugs; supplies are 220-volt. UK appliances require an adaptor, US ones a transformer.

Embassies/Consulates

If you lose your passport or need other help, contact your nearest national embassy or consulate.
Australia: Australian Consulate General, 3rd floor, Via Borgogna 2, Milan; tel: 02-7767 4200; www.italy.embassy.gov.au

Canada: Canadian Consulate, Via Zara 30, Rome; tel: 06-85444.1 (recorded info only);
email: consul.rome@international.gc.ca
New Zealand: Consulate General, Via Terraggio 17, Milan; tel: 02-4801 2577; www.nzembassy.com
Republic of Ireland: Honorary Consulate, Piazza S. Pietro in Gessate 2, Milan; tel: 02-5518 7569
UK: British Consulate General, Via San Paolo 7, Milan; tel: 02-723 001; email: Milan.ConsularEscalations@fco.gov.uk
US: US Consulate General, Via Principe Amedeo 2/10, Milan; tel: 02-290 351; www.usconsulate.gov

Emergency numbers

Ambulance: 118
Fire: 115
General emergency: 112
Police: 113

H

Health

All EU countries have reciprocal arrangements for reclaiming the costs of medical services. UK residents should obtain the EHIC (European Health Insurance Card), available from post offices or online at www.ehic.org.uk. These arrangements are all subject to change after Brexit; check these details before departing for your flight.

This only covers you for medical care, not for emergency repatriation costs or

additional expenses such as accommodation and flights for anyone travelling with you. To cover all eventualities a travel insurance policy is advisable, and for non-EU residents essential.

A pharmacy *(farmacia)* is a good first stop for medical advice. The name of the duty or all-night pharmacy is posted on pharmacy doors.

I

Internet

Most hotels offer WiFi. Charges usually apply, though some hotels offer free WiFi in public areas. WiFi is available in airports, train stations and other public places but outside the larger towns can be hard to come by. If needed, tourist offices can usually supply a list of local internet points. A passport or ID may be required for internet use.

L

Left Luggage

There are left-luggage facilities at all the airports and at Milan's Central Station. Look for the signs '*Deposito Bagagli*'.

LGBTQ travellers

Milan is Italy's gay-friendly capital, and other large towns in the region, such as Brescia, have gay bars and clubs. The Italian gay organisation, Arcigay (www. arcigay.org, only partially translated into English) has branches in Milan, Brescia, Cremona, Verona and Mantua.

Lost Property

In the event of lost valuables contact the nearest police station *(questura)*. Milan has an office for lost property *(oggetti smarriti)* at Via Friuli 30 (tel: 02-8845 3900, Italian-speaking only, Mon–Fri 8.30am–noon, 1–3.30pm), and another at Central Station within the left luggage office on the ground floor of the Galleria (6am–11pm).

M

Maps

Tourist offices can normally provide you with free town maps and sketchy regional ones. The Touring Club Italiano (TCI) publishes excellent road and hiking maps.

Media

Newspapers. English and foreign newspapers are available from kiosks of main towns and resorts. National newspapers include the Milan-based centre-right daily, *Corriere della Sera*, and its centre-left rival, *La Repubblica*.

Television and radio. Most hotels provide satellite TV, broadcasting 24-hour English-speaking news channels – but not necessarily many other channels in English. Italian TV, comprising the state-run RAI 1, 2 and 3 channels, along with a large number of private channels, churns out chat-shows, soaps, films and numerous

Santa Maria del Monte village

advertisements. The state-run radio stations, RAI 1, 2 and 3, mainly broadcast news, chat and music. For the BBC World Service check its website on www.bbc.co.uk/worldserviceradio for frequency details.

Money

Currency. The unit of currency in Italy is the euro (€), which is divided into 100 cents. Banknotes come in denominations of 500, 200, 100, 50, 20, 10 and 5 euros; coins come in 2 and 1 euros, and 50, 20, 10, 5, 2 and 1 cents.

Cash machines. The easiest way to access cash is to use an ATM *(bancomat)* with a Maestro, Cirrus, MasterCard or Visa card and PIN number. ATMs are widespread and have instructions in the main European languages.

Credit cards. Major international credit cards are accepted in most hotels, restaurants, stores and supermarkets.

Exchange offices *(cambio)*. These tend to charge more commission than banks.

Traveller's cheques. Since ATMs and credit cards have become the norm, traveller's cheques are less widely accepted.

Police

In an emergency the *Carabinieri* can be reached on 113, or you can ring the general emergency number: 112. In the case of stolen goods contact the local police station *(questura)*.

Post

Post offices normally open Mon–Fri 8.15am–2pm, Sat 8.15am–noon or 2pm. Only main post offices in major towns open all day (Mon–Fri). Stamps *(francobolli)* can also be purchased from tobacconists.

Public holidays

Shops, banks, museums and galleries usually close on the days listed below:

1 Jan New Year's Day
6 Jan Epiphany
Mar/Apr Easter
Mar/Apr Easter Monday
25 Apr Liberation Day
1 May Labour Day
2 June Republic Day
15 Aug Assumption Day
1 Nov All Saints' Day
8 Dec Feast of the Immaculate Conception
25 Dec Christmas Day
26 Dec St Stephen's Day

Religion

Like the rest of Italy, the region is primarily Roman Catholic. The Church still plays a major role in the community, although numbers of regular worshippers have been in decline for some years. Milan has congregations of all the main religions.

Windsurfer on Lake Garda

S

Smoking

Since 2005, smoking has been banned in indoor public places. This includes bars and restaurants, unless they have a separate area for smokers – which very few do.

T

Telephones

Phone numbers. Whether phoning from abroad or within Italy, the full area code must be used. Toll-free numbers within Italy that begin 800 need no other code. Numbers starting with 0 are landlines, those starting with 3 are mobiles.

Calling from abroad. To dial Italy from the UK, dial 00 (international code) + 39 (Italy) + area code + number. To call other countries from Italy, first dial the international code (00), then the country code: Australia 61, Ireland 353, UK 44, US and Canada 1.

Generally, there is an off-peak rate for international calls in Italy but the times can depend on the network you are using.

Mobile phones. EU mobile (cell) phones can be used in Italy, but check compatibility before you leave. The EU Commission has set a fixed rate for charges so the high cost of roaming has been generally made a thing of the past. Be aware this only applies to EU cell phones and mobile carriers; if you are travelling with a non-EU phone roaming charges will very much apply. It may be worth buying an Italian SIM card, available from any mobile-phone shop, if you intend to stay for more than a few weeks. The major GSM network providers are Telecom Italia Mobile (TIM), Vodafone, Wind, and H3G.

Public phone boxes. If you are lucky enough to find one of the few remaining public phones they can be operated with a card *(scheda/carta telefónica)*, available from telephone offices, tobacconists, newsstands, and vending machines; some also take credit cards. Remember to tear off the corner of the card before use. Otherwise, prepaid international telephone cards (from 5 euros), available at post offices and other outlets, can make calling abroad remarkably cheap.

Useful numbers

Directory enquiries: 12
International enquiries: 176

Time differences

Italy is one hour ahead of Greenwich Mean Time (GMT). From the last Sunday in March to the last Sunday in October, clocks are put forward an hour.

Tipping

Tipping is not taken for granted in Italy, although a bit extra will always

Limone sul Garda

be appreciated. In restaurants 5–10 percent is customary unless service has been added to the bill. For quick service in bars, leave a coin or two with your till receipt when ordering. Taxi drivers do not expect a tip, but will appreciate it if you round up the fare to the next euro.

Toilets

Public toilets are hard to come by. If you use the facilities of cafés and bars, buying a drink will be appreciated – even if it is only a glass of mineral water at the bar.

Tourist information

Around Lake Maggiore
Orta San Giulio: Via Panoramica 1.
Stresa: Piazza Marconi 16; tel: 0323-31308.
Varese: Via Carrobbio 2; tel: 0332-281 944.

Around Lake Como
Bellagio: Piazza Mazzini 48; tel: 031-950 204.
Como: Via Albertolli 7; tel: 031-304 137.
Menaggio: Piazza Garibaldi 8; tel: 0344-32924.

Around Lake Iseo
Bergamo: Via Gombito 13, Città Alta (Upper Town); tel: 035-242 226.
Orio al Serio airport, tel: 035-320 402
Iseo: Lungolago G. Marconi 2c; tel: 030-374 8733.

Around Lake Garda
Brescia: Piazza del Foro 6,; tel: 030-374 9916.
Desenzano del Garda: Via Porto Vecchio 34; tel: 030-374 8726.
Gardone Riviera: Corso Repubblica, 1; tel: 030-374 8736.
Salo: Piazza Sant'Antonio 4; tel: 030-374-8745.
Riva del Garda: Largo Medaglie d'Oro al Valor Militare 5; tel: 0464-554 444.
Sirmione: Viale Marconi 6; tel: 030-374 8721.

Milan
Piazza Castello 1; tel: 02-7740 4343.

Tourist offices abroad
(Website for all the offices is www.enit.it)
UK: Italian State Tourist Board (for all regions in the lakes except Trentino), 1 Princes Street, London W1B 8AY.
US: 630 Fifth Avenue, Suite 1965, New York, NY 10111; tel: 212-245 5618.
Canada: 110 Yonge Street, Suite 503, Toronto, Ontario M5C 1T4; tel: 416-925 4882.
Australia: 140 William Street, East Sydney, NSW 2011; tel: 2 9357 2561.

Tours and guides

Tourist offices, travel agencies and hotels can provide details of tours and guides. For excursions on the lakes consult the ferry company website www.navigazionelaghi.it. The website can be quite complicated depending

Yachts on Lake Garda   *Relaxing in Torbole*

on what you are searching for, and the ferry search function is almost unworkable, but they do offer a substantial number of reasonably priced day or half day trips from March to October for all the main lakes, occasionally with the option of a three-course lunch on board.

Transport

Arrival by air

For British travellers low-cost carrier Ryanair (www.ryanair.com) operates flights from London Stansted to Bergamo's Orio al Serio airport, easyJet (www.easyjet.com) and British Airways have regular flights from Gatwick and Heathrow respectively to Milan's Linate and Malpensa airports.

From the US there are direct flights to Milan from main cities, including New York, Miami, Atlanta, Los Angeles and San Francisco.

Airports

Malpensa. Located 50km (31 miles) northwest of Milan, Malpensa airport (www.sea-aeroportimilano.it/en) is a convenient arrival point for the lakes in the west of the region (Orta, Maggiore, Varese and Como). The airport's Terminal 1 is linked to Milan's Centrale, Garibaldi and Cardorna railway stations by the half-hourly Malpensa Express (www.malpensaexpress.it). Journey time to the centre is about 40 minutes. The Malpensa Shuttle and Malpensa Bus Express provide regular coach services to Milan's Central Station, taking 50–60 minutes.

Linate. Situated 10km (6 miles) east of Milan, Linate (www.sea-aeroporti milano.it/en) is the closest airport to the city, and handles mainly domestic and European flights. The Starfly shuttle operates a half-hourly service to Milan's Central Station, taking 25 minutes; the cheaper No. 73 bus departs every 10 minutes for Piazza Duomo in the city centre. Tickets can be bought onboard the Starfly shuttle and at automatic machines outside arrivals for the No. 73 bus.

Orio al Serio. Bergamo's Orio al Serio airport, 48km/30 miles northeast of Milan (www.sacbo.it), is convenient for the western lakes, and ideal if you are heading to Lake Iseo. The city of Bergamo is only 5km (3 miles) away, with a bus service departing to the city every half an hour. Autostradale and Terravision operate half-hourly shuttle buses to Milan's Central Station, an hour away.

Brescia, Gabriele D'Annunzio. Brescia's airport (www.aeroportobrescia.it/en) lies 20km (12.5 miles) southeast of the city. The airport is worth considering for access to Lake Garda and Lake Iseo.

Valerio Catullo/Verona-Villafranca. Verona's airport (www.aeroportoverona.it) is 15km (9.5 miles) from Verona, and is handy for the Veneto shore of Lake Garda and excursions to Brescia, Mantua and Venice. Buses depart for Vero-

Some roads are carved into the hillside

na's rail station at 5.35am, 6.30am and then every 20 minutes until 11.30pm.
Other airports. Lugano airport (www.luganoairport.ch/en) is another useful gateway to the Italian Lakes, as are Venice and Treviso.

Arrival by rail
The journey from the UK to Milan, via Paris on Eurostar (www.eurostar.com) and the overnight Thello sleeper car to Milan or Verona takes just over 14 hours to Milan, 16 to Verona. Milan and Como are well served by trains from Switzerland, Germany and France. If arriving from elsewhere in Italy, there are reliable connections from Turin, Bologna, Florence and Rome, and from within the lakes region. Detailed information on international rail routes can be found at www.seat61.com or www.raileurope-world.com.

Arrival by car
The quickest route to Milan from the UK channel ports takes a minimum of 12 hours, over a distance of 1,040km (646 miles). For route planning and for details on the cost of petrol, road tolls levied on French and Italian motorways, and the Swiss motorway road tax, visit www.viamichelin.com. Reasonable motorways *(autostrade)* and main roads link the lakes from Turin, Milan, Como, Varese, Bergamo and Brescia. But bear in mind that the city centres and ring roads can be both confusing and congested.

Tolls are levied on the motorways, but it is worth the relatively small expense to cover ground fast. When you approach the payment barrier, make sure you choose the correct lane. Lanes marked 'Carte' will accept credit cards; cash lanes are indicated with a hand holding notes and coins.

Transport within the lakes region
Boats. Operating on all the main lakes, **ferries** *(battelli)* offer the most enjoyable and leisurely way of exploring the lakes. **Hydrofoils** *(aliscafi)* or **catamarans** *(catamarani)* are faster than ferries, but more expensive and less fun as passengers are confined to the inside. Tickets for these faster services allow use on ferries but not vice versa. On popular summer routes on the main lakes, the hydrofoils fill up quickly.

Useful **car ferries** *(traghetti)* link Intra and Laveno on Lake Maggiore; Menaggio, Varenna, Cadenabbia and Bellagio on Lake Como; and Toscolano-Maderno to Torri del Benaco and Limone to Malcesine on Lake Garda.
Timetables covering all ferries and hydrofoils are available from ferry ticket offices, tourist information offices and online for the main lakes at www.navigazionelaghi.it. Timetables change at least twice a year, but the routes remain quite constant. Ferries normally run from 7am but stop quite early in the evening, and services between 12.30pm and 2.30pm are limited.

There is a bewildering variety of **tickets and deals** for the major lakes, so check the options before your first trip. These include an all-day ticket for parts or all of the lake, a single or return ferry ticket, and a ferry ticket that includes entry to (or a price reduction at) major sites. Some boats have a bar; others have a restaurant.

An all-day ticket is the most convenient option, but cost-wise it is worthwhile only for several journeys on the same day. Generally, children under the age of four travel free, four- to twelve-year-olds are just over half-price. Over-60s from the EU nations are entitled to a 20 percent reduction on weekdays (with proof of identity). Return boat tickets (excluding catamarans or hydrofoils) tend to be valid for two days.

Lake cruises. The ferry company Navigazione Lago d'Iseo (www.navigazionelagoiseo.it) not only provides an excellent boat service linking lake villages and islands but offers a variety of reasonably priced cruises during the summer season. On varying weekdays in July and August, you can take the day-tour cruise, which includes guided visits of historic lakeside villages and Monte Isola. Typically on Sundays (mid-June–7 Sept) there are short trips to all three islands. Saturday nights in season see the romantic Blue Night Cruise, with candlelit dinners and music on board.

Cruising on the Lake Garda. There are three types of boats: *Battello* ('Batt'), the regular ferry boats, the slightly speedier *Catamarano* ('Cat') and the *Servizio Rapido* ('Sr'), the fastest service, which makes fewer stops and incurs a supplement. There are also Traghetti, which are the car ferries that link Toscolano Maderno to Torri del Benaco, and Limone to Malcesine. A *biglietto di libera circolazione* allows unlimited journeys for one day; it is worth buying if you plan to make several stops. There are separate kinds for the whole lake, the lower lake or the upper lake. Services, particularly on the fast boats, are not very regular, so check timings before starting your journey.

Motorboats. Public ferry services stop early in the evening so if you want to dine in another resort, you should organise transport for the return trip. Bear in mind that private motorboats are generally far more expensive than land taxis. Some island restaurants might transport diners back to the mainland (for example, from Lake Maggiore's Isola dei Pescatori back to Stresa), others, such as Orta San Giulio and Isola Comacina, have an inexpensive boat service. If you are worried about being stranded, discuss the options with your restaurant. If you are using a motorboat taxi, negotiate a price before setting off.

Bus. A reasonably priced bus network links towns and villages along the lakeshores. If you do not have a car, a bus can be the quickest means of reaching some destinations; for example, from Stresa to Lake Orta, and (on Lake Garda) from Desenzano to Sirmione,

Young cyclists in Arco

Salò, Gardone or Limone – all of which are inaccessible by train. Services linking villages are less regular, and some stop very early in the evening.

Rail. Milan is the main rail hub for the lakes, with excellent, well-priced services to the main towns across the region. Bergamo, Stresa (Lake Maggiore) and Como (Lake Como) all take around an hour by rail. Lakes Varese and Garda (using the station at Brescia) are also well served by trains. Desenzano, on the Milan–Venice line, is the main terminal on the southern shore of Lake Garda. However, the lakes themselves are better served by ferries and buses.

Intercity, Eurocity or Eurostar trains levy a supplement of at least 30 percent, and require seat reservations. It is advisable to make a reservation well in advance. Return tickets offer no saving on two singles. Tickets must be stamped in the yellow machines on the platforms before boarding the train. Tickets bought on the train incur a hefty supplement. For information on train travel in Italy, see www.trenitalia.com or www.trenord.it.

Land taxis. Taxi fares are high, and there are additional charges for luggage in the boot (trunk), trips at night and trips on Sundays and holidays. Beware of touts without meters who may approach you at airports (especially Linate) and large train stations. The main squares of the larger towns usually have a taxi rank.

Car rental
Car-rental bookings made in advance on the internet work out cheaper than hiring on arrival. Make sure you check all the extras when comparing quotes from different companies. The major car-rental companies have offices in the main cities and airports.

Drivers must present their own national driving licence or one that is internationally recognised. There is an additional charge for an extra driver. Credit-card imprints are taken as a deposit and are usually the only form of payment acceptable. 'Inclusive' prices do not generally include personal accident insurance or insurance against damage to windscreens, tyres and wheels.

Driving
Rules of the road. Drive on the right; pass on the left. Speed limits in Italy are 50km/h (30mph) in towns and built-up areas, 90km/h (55mph) on main roads and 130km/h (80mph) on motorways. Speeding and other traffic offences are subject to heavy on-the-spot fines.

At roundabouts the traffic from the right has the right of way. Seat belts are compulsory in the front and back, and children should be properly restrained. The use of hand-held mobile telephones while driving is prohibited. The blood alcohol limit is 0.08 percent, and police occasionally make random breath tests. Lights must be used on motorways, dual carriageways and on all out-of-town roads. Visibility vests

and a warning triangle are compulsory.

Breakdowns. In case of accident or breakdown call 112 (general emergencies) or the Automobile Club of Italy (ACI) on 803116. The club has an efficient 24-hour service, which is available to foreign visitors.

Petrol. On main roads there are plenty of 24-hour stations with self-service dispensers that accept euro notes but not necessarily credit cards.

Parking. Finding a parking space in the centre of lakeside resorts is notoriously tricky. Check your hotel has parking facilities (charges can be quite high) or can recommend a parking lot nearby. Parking in towns is controlled by meters or scratch cards, available from tobacconists and bars. The larger towns have multi-storey car parks. Some free parking is controlled by parking discs (if you have hired a car a disc will be provided).

Travellers with disabilities

Steep cobbled streets, steps and some museums without wheelchair access can present challenges for disabled travellers. Specialised tour operators can offer customised tours and itineraries, eg Flying Wheels Travel (www.disabledholidays4u.com) and Accessible Journeys (www.disabilitytravel.com). Able Trader (http://www.abletrader.com/accessible_travel_links.php) is a database of travel agents and resources from around the world with experience in accessible travel. If you are going to be in Milan, visit the Milano per Tutti (Milan for All) website (www.milanopertutti.it) which provides a large amount of information for visitors with disabilities to the city.

Visas and passports

For citizens of EU countries a valid passport or identity card is all that is required to enter Italy for stays of up to 90 days. Citizens of Australia, New Zealand, the UK, and the US also require only a valid passport. For stays of over 90 days a visa or residence permit is required.

Websites

Official tourist board websites:

www.distrettolaghi.it – Lake Orta and the west of Lake Maggiore.

www.vareseturismo.it – province of Varese, including Lake Maggiore's eastern side.

www.ascona-locarno.com - Swiss Lake Maggiore.

www.turismo.regione.lombardia.it – Lombardy.

www.lakecomo.com – Lake Como.

www.bresciaholiday.com – Lake Iseo, Franciacorta, lower Lake Garda.

www.visitgarda.com – Lake Garda.

www.visitamilano.it – Milan.

Weights and measures

The metric system is used for all weights and measures in Italy.

Italians are easy–going

LANGUAGE

Italian is relatively easy to pick up, if you have any knowledge of French or Spanish (or a grounding in Latin). Most hotels have staff who speak some English, and unless you go well off the beaten track, you should have little problem communicating in shops or restaurants. However, there are places not on the tourist circuit where you will have the chance to practise your Italian, and local people will think more of you for making an effort. Here are a few basics to help you get started.

Useful phrases

General
Yes *Sì*
No *No*
Thank you *Grazie*
Many thanks *Mille grazie/Tante grazie*
You're welcome *Prego*
All right/That's fine *Va bene*
Please *Per favore/Per cortesia*
Excuse me (to get attention) *Scusi*
Excuse me (in a crowd) *Permesso*
Could you help me? (formal) *Potrebbe aiutarmi?*
Certainly *Ma, certo/Certamente*
Can you show me...? *Può indicarmi...?*
Can you help me, please? *Può aiutarmi, per cortesia?*
I need... *Ho bisogno di...*
I'm lost *Mi sono perso*

I'm sorry *Mi dispiace*
I don't know *Non lo so*
I don't understand *Non capisco*
Do you speak English/French/Spanish? *Parla inglese/francese/spagnolo?*
Could you speak more slowly? *Può parlare più lentamente, per favore?*
Could you repeat that please? *Può ripetere, per piacere?*
How much does it cost? *quanto costa?*
this one/that one *questo/quello*
Have you got...? *Avete...?*

At a bar/restaurant
I'd like to book a table *Vorrei prenotare un tavolo*
Have you got a table for...? *Avete un tavolo per...?*
I have a reservation *Ho prenotato*
lunch/supper *il pranzo/la cena*
I'm a vegetarian *Sono vegetariano/a*
May we have the menu? *Ci dia la carta?*
What would you like? *Che cosa prende?*
I'd like... *Vorrei...*
mineral water fizzy/still *acqua minerale gasata/naturale*
a bottle of *una bottiglia di*
a glass of *un bicchieri di*
red/white wine *vino rosso/bianco*
beer *una birra*

Numbers
One *uno*

Try and mingle   *Practise your Italian at any opportunity*

Two *due*
Three *tre*
Four *quattro*
Five *cinque*
Six *sei*
Seven *sette*
Eight *otto*
Nine *nove*
Ten *dieci*
Twenty *venti*
Thirty *trenta*
Forty *quaranta*
Fifty *cinquanta*
One hundred *cento*
One thousand *mille*

Getting around
What time do you open/close? *A che ora apre/chiude?*
Closed for the holidays *Chiuso per ferie*
Where can I buy tickets? *Dove posso fare i biglietti?*
What time does the train leave? *A che ora parte il treno?*
Can you tell me where to get off? *Mi può dire dove devo scendere?*
Where is the nearest bank/hotel? *Dov'è la banca/l'albergo più vicino?*
On the right *a destra*
On the left *a sinistra*
Go straight on *Va sempre diritto*

Online
Where's an internet cafe? *Dov'è un Internet caffè?*
Does it have wireless internet? *C'è il wireless?*

What is the WiFi password? *Qual è la password WiFi?*
Is the WiFi free? *Il WiFi è gratis?*
How do I turn the computer on/off? *Come si accende/spegne il computer?*
Can I...? *Posso...?*
access the internet *collegarmi (a Internet)*
check e-mail *controllare le e-mail*
print *stampare*
plug in/charge my laptop/iPhone/iPad? *collegare/ricaricare il mio portatile/iPhone/iPad?*
access Skype? *usare Skype?*
How much per hour/half hour? *Quanto costa per un'ora/mezz'ora?*
How do I...? *Come...?*
connect/disconnect *ci si collega/scollega*
log on/log off *si fa il login/logout*
What's your e-mail? *Qual è la sua e-mail?*
My e-mail is... *La mia e-mail è...*

Social media
Are you on Facebook/Twitter? *È su Facebook/Twitter? (polite form) Sei su Facebook/Twitter? (informal form)*
What's your user name? *Qual è il suo nome utente? (polite form) Qual è il tuo nome utente? (informal form)*
I'll add you as a friend. *La aggiungerò come amico. (polite form) Ti aggiungerò come amico. (informal form)*
I'll follow you on Twitter. *La seguirò su Twitter. (polite form) Ti seguirò su Twitter. (informal form)*

George Clooney and Vincent Cassel in 'Ocean's Twelve'

BOOKS AND FILM

Introduction

The sight of sluggish steamers and snow-clad peaks stirs something deep in most visitors, but especially in the souls of poets. It is of little coincidence that two of the most romantic Roman poets, Virgil and Catullus, came from the lakes and were inspired by the seductive setting. Pliny, too, loved the lakes. Later, the Romantics fell in love with the region. 'This lake exceeds anything I ever beheld in beauty,' declared Shelley of Lake Como, exploring the lake in 1818. Novelist Edith Wharton, visiting in 1903, was intoxicated by the Romantic poets' visions of brooding lakes. The German poet and dramatist Goethe was drawn to Lake Garda by its classical resonance, even if it was the lemons rather than the literature that won his heart. 'What I enjoy most of all is the fruit,' he wrote in his journal in 1786. He had less fondness for Malcesine, where the Austrian police, spotting him sketching the castle, arrested him on suspicion of being a spy.

Since the 18th century, Lake Garda's summer villas have lured such luminaries as Byron and D.H. Lawrence. Lawrence said of Limone, describing is 'as beautiful as the beginning of creation'. Ibsen and Vladimir Nabokov concurred, even if their preference was for the greater Gardone Riviera.

'One can't describe the beauty of the Italian lakes, nor would one try if one could,' wrote Henry James, on catching sight of Lake Maggiore. Such outpourings of purple prose, particularly from writers fleeing northern climes, are part of the lakes' legacy.

Books

Travel companions

Desiring Italy, Susan Cahill (ed). Writings by female authors (George Eliot, Edith Wharton, Muriel Spark, etc) on the beauty and culture of Italy.

Italian Days, Barbara Grizutti Harrison. A witty and eloquent look at Italy, revealing a fascinating insight into a nation.

History, society and culture

A History of Contemporary Italy: Society and Politics: 1943–1988, Italy and Its Discontents, 1980–2001 and Silvio Berlusconi: Television, Power and Patrimony, Paul Ginsborg – A masterly history of post-war Italy and its politics is completed with an account of the power of the country's most powerful politician.

Alps and Sanctuaries, Samuel Butler. The 18th-century traveller describes his journeys around the lakes.

Mussolini, Nicholas Farrell. A biography of the reviled Fascist dictator that pulls no punches. It includes the period of the Salò Republic, when Mussolini's power-base was on the shores of Lake Garda.

Villas make for a fabulous backdrop

The House of Gucci, Sarah Forden. A biography of Maurizio Gucci, the last family member to run the luxury-goods fashion empire.

The Dark Heart of Italy, Tobias Jones. Although flawed and obsessed with a Berlusconi era that is now history, this is an intriguing look at the underbelly of Italy, from politics, crime and (lack of) punishment to the Italian way of life.

How the English Made the Alps, Jim Ring. The English love affair with the Alps, from its beginnings in the early Romantic movement, through to its Victorian heyday.

La Bella Figura, Beppe Severgnini. Incisive tour behind the seductive face that Italy puts on for visitors by a columnist for the daily newspaper *Corriere della Sera*.

Fiction and travelogue

A Farewell to Arms, Ernest Hemingway. The novel tells the story of a wounded American soldier in the Italian army who convalesces in Milan, inadvertently deserts while fleeing from the Germans but is reunited with his beloved in Stresa, on Lake Maggiore.

Europa, Italian Neighbours, A Season With Verona, Tim Parks. The novelist observes life in Italy in a series of light-hearted and affectionate tales.

Food and wine

Eating up Italy: Voyages on a Vespa, Matthew Fort. Exploring Italy's regions on an epic scooter trip, Matthew Fort paints a contemporary portrait of Italy through its food and the people who produce it.

Truly Italian, Ursula Ferrigno. An Italian cookbook with inspirational recipes and a vegetarian focus that features the healthiest northern Italian cooking.

Film

This beautiful area has inspired a number of films, of which the following is a selection:

A Month on the Lake (1995). This film, starring Vanessa Redgrave and Uma Thurman, is just one of many featuring Lake Como's magnificent Villa del Balbianello.

Star Wars Episode II: Attack of the Clones (2002). Villa del Balbianello features again, this time as planet Naboo, where the wedding of Anakin Skywalker (Darth Vader) and Padmé Amidala is held.

Ocean's Twelve (2004). George Clooney's attachment to Lake Como has led to films including this one, in which he stars, being filmed in the region. Villa Erba is used as the home of François Toulour, the Night Fox.

Casino Royale (2006). Parts of the acclaimed first James Bond film with Daniel Craig in the title role were filmed on Lake Como. Bond finds Mr White at his estate on the lake, Villa La Gaeta, and Villa del Balbianello is used as the sanatorium where Bond recuperates after being tortured by Le Chiffre.

Quantum of Solace (2008). Craig's second Bond film includes a car chase around Lake Garda.

ABOUT THIS BOOK

This *Explore Guide* has been produced by the editors of Insight Guides, whose books have set the standard for visual travel guides since 1970. With top-quality photography and authoritative recommendations, these guidebooks bring you the very best routes and itineraries in the world's most exciting destinations.

BEST ROUTES

The routes in the book provide something to suit all budgets, tastes and trip lengths. As well as covering the destination's many classic attractions, the itineraries track lesser-known sights, and there are also excursions for those who want to extend their visit outside the city. The routes embrace a range of interests, so whether you are an art fan, a gourmet, a history buff or have kids to entertain, you will find an option to suit.

We recommend reading the whole of a route before setting out. This should help you to familiarise yourself with it and enable you to plan where to stop for refreshments – options are shown in the 'Food and Drink' box at the end of each tour.

For our pick of the tours by theme, consult Recommended Routes for… (see pages 6–7).

INTRODUCTION

The routes are set in context by this introductory section, giving an overview of the destination to set the scene, plus background information on food and drink, shopping and more, while a succinct history timeline highlights the key events over the centuries.

DIRECTORY

Also supporting the routes is a Directory chapter, with a clearly organised A–Z of practical information, our pick of where to stay while you are there and select restaurant listings; these eateries complement the more low-key cafés and restaurants that feature within the routes and are intended to offer a wider choice for evening dining. Also included here are some nightlife listings, plus a handy language guide and our recommendations for books and films about the destination.

ABOUT THE AUTHORS

Susie Boulton has travelled extensively in Italy for over 25 years, and has written and contributed to many of Insight's Italian titles. Susie first became acquainted with the Italian Lakes while working for *Holiday Which?* magazine, providing information on the cleanliness of lake waters, comfort of hotels and quality of regional cuisine. More recently, she wrote the Berlitz Pocket Guides to both Milan and the Italian Lakes. Whether for work or pleasure, Susie finds any excuse to revisit this sublime region of northern Italy.

Many of the tours in this book were originally conceived by Italy specialist Lisa Gerard-Sharp. Thanks also go to Clare Peel.

CONTACT THE EDITORS

We hope you find this Explore Guide useful, interesting and a pleasure to read. If you have any questions or feedback on the text, pictures or maps, please do let us know. If you have noticed any errors or outdated facts, or have suggestions for places to include on the routes, we would be delighted to hear from you. Please drop us an email at hello@insightguides.com. Thanks!

CREDITS

Explore Italian Lakes
Editor: Zara Sekhavati
Author: Susie Boulton
Head of DTP and Pre-Press: Rebeka Davies
Update Production: Apa Digital
Managing Editor: Carine Tracanelli
Picture Editor: Tom Smyth
Cartography: original cartography
Berndston & Berndston, updated by Carte
Photo credits: 123RF 8MC, 32, 40/41, 62,
100, 124/125; Alamy 44/45; Apa Publications 7MR, 16/17, 18/19; AWL Images 1,
4/5T; Corbis 102/103T; Dreamstime 20/21,
22, 31, 33, 46, 47L, 50/51, 67, 68, 69L,
82/83, 83L, 84, 118/119, 137; Fotolia 6ML,
22/23, 36, 38, 39L, 40, 41L, 55L, 60/61,
63, 68/69, 76, 77, 79, 80/81, 84/85; Getty
Images 26; Glyn Genin/Apa Publications
17L, 70/71, 71L, 72, 72/73, 73L, 100/101,
101L, 120; Grand Hotel des Iles Borromées
104, 105; Grand Hotel Villa Serbelloni 114,
114/115, 115L; iStockphoto 6MC, 7MR,
14/15, 25, 28MR, 28ML, 34, 35, 37L, 42,
48, 48/49, 49L, 52, 53L, 54, 54/55, 64,
66, 70, 74/75, 82, 86, 122, 123, 127,
128/129, 130; Leonardo 102MR, 102ML,
106, 106/107, 107L, 108, 108/109, 109L,
112, 113, 116, 117; Mockford & Bonetti/Apa
Publications 28ML, 28MC, 28MC, 36/37,
38/39, 46/47, 56, 57L, 91L, 102MR; Neil
Buchan-Grant/Apa Publications 4ML, 4MC,
4MR, 4MR, 4MC, 4ML, 6BC, 7T, 7M, 8ML,
8ML, 8MC, 8MR, 8MR, 10, 11, 12, 12/13,
13L, 16, 18, 19L, 21L, 23L, 24, 28MR, 30,
42/43, 43L, 52/53, 56/57, 58, 59, 60, 61L,
64/65, 65L, 78, 80, 81L, 87, 88, 88/89,
89L, 90, 90/91, 92, 92/93, 93L, 94, 95, 96,
97, 102ML, 102MC, 102MC, 110, 110/111,
111L, 121, 126, 128, 129L, 131, 132, 133,
134, 134/135, 135L; Public Domain 6TL,
98/99; Robert Harding 8/9T, 20, 28/29T;
Terme di Sirmione 85L; The Kobal Collection
136; TopFoto 27
Cover credits: iStock (main&bottom)

Printed by CTPS – China

DISTRIBUTION

UK, Ireland and Europe
Apa Publications (UK) Ltd
sales@insightguides.com
United States and Canada
Ingram Publisher Services
ips@ingramcontent.com
Australia and New Zealand
Woodslane
info@woodslane.com.au
Southeast Asia
Apa Publications (Singapore) Pte
singaporeoffice@insightguides.com
Worldwide
Apa Publications (UK) Ltd
sales@insightguides.com

SPECIAL SALES, CONTENT LICENSING AND COPUBLISHING

Insight Guides can be purchased in bulk
quantities at discounted prices. We can
create special editions, personalised
jackets and corporate imprints tailored to
your needs.
sales@insightguides.com
www.insightguides.biz

INDEX